THE GIRLPRINT

The ultimate blueprint for girls to propel their dreams into action

---

Valeisha Butterfield Jones
with
LaMonique Hamilton

The Girlprint
Copyright © 2014 by HEIRLIGHT

First published by Heirlight, a division of Heirlight, LLC
First Heirlight paperback edition May 2014

For more information on special discounts for bulk purchases, please contact info@heirlight.com. To book an event or an author, please contact the Heirlight Speakers Bureau at booking@heirlight.com.

LIBRARY OF CONGRESS CATALOGING-IN-PUBLICATION DATA:
Jones, Valeisha Butterfield
The Girlprint: The ultimate blueprint for girls to propel their dreams into action/Valeisha Butterfield Jones; with LaMonique Hamilton.
p. cm.   v2.

ISBN 978-0-692-02625-0

1. Women – life skills guides – self-esteem.
2. Career
3. Dreams.
4. Jones, Valeisha Butterfield.

I. Hamilton, LaMonique.
II. Title.
XXXXXXXXXXXXXXXX

Printed in the United States of America
10   9   8   7   6   5   4   3   2   1

I am thankful to my loving husband, Dahntay Jones, and our beautiful sons Dahntay and Tanner Jones, for their unconditional love and for encouraging me to be the best wife, mom and businesswoman that I can possibly be.

To Jean Farmer Butterfield, G. K. Butterfield and Odell Sharpe Farmer, for without your unwavering love, support and solid foundation, this story could not be told.

I am thankful to the countless teachers, mentors, family members and friends who believed in me and, most importantly, God for giving me the courage to dream big and the will to make those dreams come true.

Contents

Introduction

We were not born to be average and, as children, we are taught to believe that anything is possible. However, as life takes its course and the bills start piling up, many of us, especially young women, lose confidence and because of fear, defer our dreams.

This book is not intended for the faint of heart. To follow your dreams you must prepare for war and be willing to fight on the front lines of your own success. By war, in this case, I am not referring to the struggles of growing up in a single parent home or not having food on the table, but what I am referring to is self-induced struggle. Having the option of accepting a cozy job with a corner office or becoming a career student to prolong entering into the real world, but rather taking the road less traveled. I'm referring to a passion that burns so deep in your soul that you can't ignore it. A calling that speaks so loudly that you cannot concentrate on anything else, but the purpose God has placed on your heart.

Most people, including close family and friends will not understand your dreams. In fact, they may even laugh in your face or smirk behind your back. Growing up in a small town with dreams bigger than my surroundings, I had nowhere to turn for advice and felt very alone. We were taught to follow the status quo of becoming a lawyer, doctor or teacher. And while they are all respectable professions, they were not for me and I knew this from a very early age. The idea of wanting to work in the entertainment industry was a foreign concept to my parents and teachers, one that they couldn't comprehend. My friends gave me blank stares. There was no foothold to what I wanted to do where I was, so having that particular goal meant that I would have to leave my family, friends, and everything I knew in order to pursue my dreams. *Don't expect people to understand your grind when God didn't give them your vision.*

Living a purpose-driven life is something that isn't taught at home or in an academic setting. Society has programmed us to believe that receiving a formal education and landing a good-paying job with a nice benefits package is enough. While in theory this makes perfect sense, why settle for a job that you must pull yourself out of bed each morning to perform just to make ends meet?

If you're anything like me, and I assume that you are because you purchased this book, you refuse to live a mediocre life full of meaningless jobs and passionless work for a paycheck. You want to make a *life* for yourself and not just a living.

In this book, you will find solace in knowing that you are not alone. Through my journey, my hope is that you find peace in knowing that your dreams are valid and attainable if you're willing to sacrifice and put in the work. The journey will not be easy, but nothing worth having ever is.

CHAPTER ONE

The Audacity To Dream

*"There is no passion to be found playing small,
in settling for a life that is less than the one you are
capable of living."*

– Nelson Mandela

It's 7:45 a.m. and a white hot 1985 smoke-filled Chevy Camaro is parked outside of my parent's home. Each morning, Aunt Joyce honked the horn two times and yelled, "Come on girls!" as my sister and I ran outside and jumped into the car. I immediately transformed into a different person on my way to elementary school.

Behind the walls of our two story brick home and perfectly manicured lawn in Wilson, North Carolina, was what appeared to be the ideal Black American family. With enough degrees, world travel and Greek affiliations to cover a small village, we were considered the *real* Huxtables and my sister and I were expected to act, talk and think accordingly. That was until Aunt Joyce picked us up from home each morning and allowed us to be us. She was my mother's sister and lived on "the other" side of town. She was just about as real and genuine as it gets. We were able to express ourselves and quickly changed our hairstyles and outfits in the car, listening to whatever was out on the radio until we pulled up to the school steps.

Our house on Vance Street was quiet most of the time. Inside, love and law permeated the air—the sound of my clarinet squeaking as I attempted to learn how to play broke the order, the pattern, and the silence. My parents, both of whom are public servants, had mapped out a bright future for me, and I knew nothing more than to live in their vision and follow their roadmap. Outside of my door, more of the same. Quiet. A safe neighborhood on the "right" side of town, the side where people aspired to be something great. However, only a mile or two away, people were destitute and often stricken with desperation. They longed for much more, if only they could get unstuck from that cycle of poverty, lack of education and resources that plagued our town. I knew them because my parents fought for them everyday. We lived in one of the poorest districts in the nation, and while I grew up with opportunities most of my friends didn't have, my parents never missed a chance to remind me that we were the same. Attending public school was one of the best gifts I could have ever received. It taught me the importance of humility and exposed me to the real struggles our communities faced each day.

But I didn't live there. I lived among professional people, and played with kids who had bunnies as pets. I was content in my eleven-year-old quiet life, until another Black family moved into the neighborhood and their thirteen-year-old son Antonio brought a cassette tape into our home that would forever color my world. He introduced me to *The Great Adventures of Slick Rick*.

I fell in love. The lyrics, the beat, the cadence and the immediacy of hip-hop filled me, where before there had only been silence. I was a pre-teen obsessed. I absorbed everything that played on Channel 27 – BET – and watched Channel 18 – MTV – religiously for *Yo!* MTV Raps and later Big Tigger's Tha Basement. My parents didn't approve of me listening to the music, so I went to friends' and relatives' homes to invade their extensive catalogues of hip-hop and listened to my heart's content. Hip-hop became my secret *passion*.

This was my first real moment of clarity. There was the feeling that I had found a key puzzle piece of my life. To me, hip-hop felt more authentic, more gritty and more real than anything I had experienced before. It personified not necessarily my life, but the world surrounding me. Life wasn't perfect and hip-hop illustrated that. Everything about hip-hop fit who I was and who I longed to be. You'll find that when we reach these moments of clarity, they are life-altering. However scary they may be or fleeting they may feel, perhaps that alteration is needed and correct.

In my case, this clarity came as my seemingly perfect family was falling apart. My parents weren't getting along and it had been that way for some time. They were both unhappy, so much so that I was relieved when my dad drove me down the street to a small split-level apartment and told me that he would be living there. Instead of feeling shattered or as if I were to blame, somehow in that moment I felt relieved. Even as an eighth grader, I realized life was too short to be unhappy and more than anything, I wanted happiness for my parents and for myself. No doubt that my newfound interest helped me process the divorce of my parents and the transition of my family. My family no longer looked "perfect," but we were much happier. Learning to trust that inner voice and those small pieces of clarity will combine with other blazingly pure moments from our daily living to form a complete vision and *dream*. Clarity of thought and clearness of the mind, allows us to push forward even when circumstances seem, at best, murky.

CHAPTER TWO

The Blueprint

"Cherish your visions and your dreams as they are the children of your soul; the blueprints of your ultimate achievements."

– Napoleon Hill

I grew older, and while I may have been a self-proclaimed hip-hop aficionado, academically I was average at best. School was not my priority, and teachers didn't hold my attention. My high school was like most schools in the South – football and basketball ruled, and everything else paled in their glory. While I was fairly well known among teachers and students, I was awkward, a tomboy and coasting. While no category for it existed, chances are I would have been voted "Least likely to succeed" if judged by my academic performance alone.

Surprisingly, my parents weren't demanding in this respect. They wanted me to try my best, but didn't expect or require me to be a 'straight A' student. I think they realized fairly early that I wasn't a traditional learner, although they wanted me to learn how to navigate in a traditional learning environment. In my case, that meant going to public school. Public school gave me a reality check of the community in which I lived. I had to learn to interact with people of different races, different socio-economic backgrounds, different religions or people of no religion at all.

Going to public school in the South in the 1980s and 1990s, I was somewhat of an anomaly. I was African-American, one generation removed from the Jim Crow South and yet still confronting many of its vestiges on a regular basis. I not only came from a family that was college-educated, I also had grandparents who were college-educated. I was solidly middle class.

And while clearly African-American, many thought I was bi-racial due in large part to my parent's background and my Bermudian heritage. Because of this, in school, I had friends, but not a particular group where I seemed to fit in. I had to learn to deal with everyone. At first, the Black students ridiculed me for my light complexion while white students made it clear that I was not one of them. The teachers, who were predominantly white, sometimes spoke in a language of social clubs and weekend gatherings that I did not understand, all while my white counterparts nodded in agreement. I had to find my way through the confusion and learned early on to find my own lane.

Still, I had moments when I cared what other people thought of me. I let it bother me. High school often felt like a popularity contest, and with no particular group to fit into, it was a contest that I could not win. At the time, I didn't realize that not "fitting in" was actually to my advantage. Being able to interact and deal with all types of people would serve me well in the years to come. I credit my grandmother for showing me the light in that respect. One day, as I bemoaned the arduous task of being a teenager, she simply said, "Let them run their mouths, while you run your business." That sentence completely shifted my mindset. While I still had and have moments of insecurity regarding how others perceive me, I know that I have to do what I need to do to best take care of me. Their words don't determine my future.

I enjoyed my high school years. Well, that was until I turned sixteen. Fresh out of the DMV with my brand new drivers license, I was ready to hit the football games. I cared less about football and more about taking my mom's Mercedes Benz for a spin. After getting ready for the game at our rival school, my mom handed over her car keys to me, but with hesitation. My best friend Dana and I took off. As we walked into the game all eyes were on me. Not because of the car or newfound driving privileges, but because of my new haircut.

"Valeisha Butterfield is bald-headed."

I kept walking, but it grew louder.

"Valeisha Butterfield is bald-headed. I know you hear me bitch!"

When I glanced over to see the source of all the commotion, I was surprised when I recognized their faces. Three girls, whom I had always been relatively cool with, suddenly became my arched-nemesis. Could a haircut be that serious? Why were they singling me out? As I continued to walk, people began to stare and laugh. I decided to leave the game. As I put the car into reverse, the screeching sound of another car stopped me in my tracks. The same girls had taken their beef with me outside. To the parking lot. A place that no longer had the safety of school security and parents. I started blowing the horn. I felt like a complete sucker, but I didn't want any problems.

Not wanting the attention, the girls sped away. As I breathed a sigh of relief, I pulled off. But the after game hotspot was the local McDonald's and I still felt compelled to go. While I knew I was taking a risk, I went anyway, wanting my night to continue before my 10:00 p.m. curfew. I parked, spoke to a few friends and got into the line to order some fries.

"What you going to do now bitch?"

Clearly going to McDonald's was a mistake. The largest one in the crew now wanted me. Bad. Refusing to give her any eye contact, I got my fries and walked away. We pulled off, but there was one small problem. I could not return my mom's car to her without gas. We were on empty and I made a stop at a nearby gas station to put a few dollars in the tank. My new beef followed us to the gas station and began antagonizing me outside of the car. I tried my best to tune it out until the glass of a Snapple bottle met the glass of my mom's windshield. In that moment, I heard the glass shatter and I snapped. I opened the door and without any further thought, I began swinging on anyone and everyone responsible. While I connected a few punches, they connected more. Instead of going home to my mom, I went to my dad's house with a black eye, a busted nose and four deep vertical scratches down my left cheek. They got exactly what they wanted.

While I had encountered people who didn't like me for one reason or another before, this was my first real glimpse at how far hate, jealousy and ignorance could go. The idea that these negative feelings could escalate into physical violence was now a reality in my life. As my physical wounds healed, I made a decision to transform the emotional scars from that incident into an education of self. Who would I be in difficult situations? How would I carry myself? Also, I wondered what I could do to help girls like us – yes, *us* – because we were all learning how to navigate our way through a tough world. Every girl in that fight wanted to win.

Sixteen also brought a new element into my life -- my first crush, Ben. He was quiet and extremely smart, and always kind to me. However, he was a high school dropout and spent time around people who were known to have illegal dealings. Ben had a deep mahogany tone, full lips, locks nearly to his waist and his pants hung low. My parents did not approve. Still, at our core, we were a lot alike and developed genuine feelings for one another. He captured a special place in my heart. But he was still a teenage boy, and he wanted what it seemed like every teenage boy was getting from their girlfriends, and I wasn't ready. He would ask, and I would make excuses. He would make promises to be gentle and loving. I would say that I had work to do. He told me that it would only take a few minutes. Pause – what? I might not have known anything about sex, but I knew that didn't sound right. I knew I deserved to have time and not be rushed. I knew that I needed to wait until I could have everything I deserved. Eventually, time and our differences took their toll on the relationship, and our brief, sweet romance was over. While I spent my daytime hours in school, Ben spent his days walking the streets.

While there was no doubt that I was privileged in many respects, my parents were never the kind of people who gave me everything I wanted. I was always expected to work and earn those things on my own. One of my first jobs while in high school was in our local mall, which was little more than an indoor shopping center, at Foot Locker. I enjoyed that job, and started learning and developing an interest in sneakers. Interestingly, my first encounter with a celebrity happened while I was working at that retail job in my small hometown. A well-known singer/songwriter, who was extremely popular at the time, had come into the store with his two sons. His wife had family in our community, and it became almost customary to hear about the "celebrity sighting" among the locals. I was a huge fan, and was so excited that it was finally my turn to see him. I was star-struck. He asked me if I could get him a shoe to try on, and I took my chance and asked him if he was the singer in question. He looked at me, and with an arrogant laugh said, "Nah, I'm Michael Jackson." Then he dismissed me, and he and his sons laughed at me as they walked out of the store. I was furious. I had no idea what the future held for me, but I vowed to never again be star-struck by anyone. Celebrities are just human, and just because they share their talents do not mean that they are relatable or even nice. I ran into the same singer years later, when his star was not quite as bright and I was on the rise in my career. I spoke to him and told him of our first encounter, to which he replied, "And your point is?" He was still arrogant and rude – until later that evening when he realized who I was and my position. Then he attempted to make amends. Too little, too late. He meant to be negative, but that encounter with him at sixteen ended up being a positive in my life, because I learned how to carry myself so that I would never again be carried.

I worked hard, but I made time to enjoy myself as a teenager. My friends and I were excited about the premier social event of high school – prom. We decided to throw an after party to get our feet wet in the party planning business and to make some money. We found a venue, sold tickets, and recruited our parents as chaperones. I was getting excited about going to the prom. I didn't have a boyfriend at the time, but one of my guy friends and I decided to be each other's date. We made all the arrangements, and along with my girlfriends and their dates, rented a limousine for the night. On the evening of the prom, I got dressed, came downstairs and waited for my date. My friends and their dates arrived, and I was still waiting. The limo drove up, and still no date. Finally, my dad called my date's parents to find out why he was so late, and found out that he had gone to the prom at another school with another girl. I couldn't believe it. I wasn't interested in him as a boyfriend, so I wasn't crushed, but I was hurt and embarrassed. I had been betrayed by someone I believed to be my friend. In that moment, I thought of Ben. I had just spoken with him the week prior. I was driving, and saw him walking down the street. He waved me over and I stopped to chat. He apologized for pressuring me to be intimate when that clearly was not something I was ready for. He said he wished he could take it back. I did too, but it was over and we had both moved on. However, his apology meant so much to me. It reassured me that I had not made a mistake by becoming involved with him, and that underneath that rough exterior was a genuine, sincere heart.

I wished I had invited Ben instead, but I decided to put on a brave face and go to the prom anyway. As I watched my friends and their dates in the limo, I kept reminding myself that I deserved to have a good time at my prom.

The prom ended up being okay, but our after party was nuts. Everyone showed up. The kids were all having a great time, and we made a good profit after our expenses were paid. The night had turned around. In the midst of our celebration, a familiar face began walking in my direction. It was one of Ben's friends. He came up to me with a strange look in his eyes and simply said, "Ben's dead yo," and walked away. I was in shock. I took in his words, and then scanned the room to find my dad. I told him what the guy said and asked him to call the police to find out if his words were true. My dad made a couple of calls, and came back to confirm that my first crush had been shot and killed in cold blood. I was devastated.

The murder rate in our town, due to gang violence, poverty, lack of opportunity, and an overall feeling of being stuck, rivaled that of a much larger city. In one year, four of my friends were murdered. Over and over, the life and potential of young people was cut short by gunfire. I was receiving quite an education, one that can only be gained by living, by experiencing things that hurt us, shake us, and break us down in the hope that we are rebuilt with empathy and understanding for one another.

During my junior year, I had a mandatory meeting with my guidance counselor, who was also the assistant principal, to discuss my plans after graduation. The only thing I knew for certain was that I was going to college and that I wanted to work in the entertainment business. So, I was surprised when she looked over my transcript and started to laugh.

"Ms. Butterfield, there's no way you're going to college. You will not be admitted with these grades. Your best bet is to go to a community college and learn a trade."

Was she serious? How could I go home and tell my educated and successful parents that my grades were only good enough to get me into trade school? I knew I needed to go to college if I had any shot of escaping the violence in my small town and somehow getting into the entertainment business, and this woman was sitting and laughing in my face, all while derailing my dreams.

"Let your dreams be bigger than your fears and your actions louder than your words."

– Unknown

Fear and doubt began to set in. She was older than me, had been through life moments that I had yet to encounter, and was trained to let students know where and how they would fit into society. What she told me was almost the polar opposite of the value of higher education instilled in me by my parents practically since birth, and the passion I had for music and entertainment. Perhaps I had been thinking too big. After all, I didn't live in a major city. I lived in a small rural town. I had watched people struggle to move away and somehow improve their circumstances and ultimately fail, settling for a life less than what they desired and convincing themselves it was comfortable. Perhaps this would also be my fate. My guidance counselor certainly seemed to believe it to be so. Her words scared me. Her laughter scared me. I had a decision to make in that moment that would alter my entire life. I decided that I was going to do exactly what she said I could not do. I now had something to prove, not only to that guidance counselor, but to my parents, my teachers, and mostly, myself.

I went home and had that difficult conversation with my parents, and together we put a plan in place to ensure that I would attend a four-year university. That plan included my parents hiring a tutor for me in my weakest subjects, math and science, and pulling my grades up to at least 2.5 GPA, which would get me into a school somewhere. I also applied to about fifteen schools, tiered as very likely, somewhat likely, and not very likely to be accepted. I adhered to the plan, and got accepted to a few schools. However, one day on a routine trip to the mailbox to look for acceptance letters, I received a crushing note from my top school, Clark Atlanta University.

Ms. Butterfield,

Thank you for applying to Clark Atlanta University. The applications process is a competitive one and we regret to inform you that your acceptance has been denied.

Crushed is an understatement. I was devastated and I began to feel my dreams slip away. Atlanta was my ticket to the entertainment industry and I thought Clark would be my vehicle to get there, but I was wrong. Instead, my parents and I agreed that I would attend North Carolina Central University in Durham, a historically Black college with an outstanding reputation, but still in North Carolina. My parents had gone there for undergraduate and law school. They knew I would receive a quality education, but I knew my dreams would be deferred.

A month before I was scheduled to leave for NCCU, my bags were packed, but I had zero enthusiasm to begin my college career. All of my acceptance letters (and rejections) were in, but something in my spirit kept leading me back to the mailbox each day. I received another letter from Clark. There had been a mistake, they apologized for the mix up and informed me that I had actually been accepted. Before jumping for joy, I first wanted to make sure my parents did not pull any strings to get me in. They assured me that they didn't and I was elated. I quickly changed my plans and began to prepare for my new life in The A. I knew that I was escaping the statistics of my small town and going to the hub of hip-hop music.

CHAPTER THREE

The Education

*"A job you can quit, a dream you can give up on,
but a calling you will chase forever."*

– Unknown

When I arrived at Hartsfield – Jackson Atlanta International Airport in August 1996 and unexpectedly stood next to rap group sensation Kris Kross at baggage claim, I knew I was one step closer to my dreams. However, as excited as I was, I was still a bit shy and nervous about making friends. My mom made it a point to connect me with five students that she felt would be good for me during my orientation. I was embarrassed, yet she was determined and persistent. Perhaps it was mother's intuition, but she was more than right. My newfound friends and I quickly formed an unbreakable bond. We talked about our dreams. We talked about guys. And we talked hip-hop and who was the best rapper, Biggie, Jay-Z or Nas. Those friendships were built solidly and endure to this day.

In addition to the studying I did for my classes, I also studied the *business* of hip-hop. My dorm room was filled with Nas, Tribe Called Quest and Mobb Deep posters. Each day, I carefully examined their album covers searching for the A&R's, product managers, attorneys and writers of those projects. I wanted to get any glimpse that I could into the world I wanted to enter.

One of the groups I studied was Wu-Tang Clan. I found out through their album cover that they had a clothing store in Atlanta called Wu Wear. I knew that getting a job there could be my foot in the door to the entertainment industry. One day, after class, I decided to make my way to their store. It was on Peachtree, and I figured that it couldn't be too far. I could walk. Little did I know that Peachtree is the main artery of the streets of Atlanta, and basically runs the length of the city. Three hours later, I was still walking. It was getting dark. I was still very unfamiliar with the city and I had two dollars to my name. I wanted to go back to the comfort of campus and my dorm, but after walking several miles already, I knew I had no choice but to press forward.

"Follow your instincts.
That's where true wisdom manifests itself"

– Oprah Winfrey

I remembered why I decided to move to Atlanta. Walking away from the comfort of what was familiar took me in the direction of opportunity. When we fail to move outside of our norm, we don't allow ourselves to grow. We linger, and ultimately decline. We have to make room for our dreams, our vision for our life by taking steps, in my case literally, that move us outside of our everyday routine. The more we move, the more God moves. The more steps we take, the more He increases our territory. There are people outside of what we immediately see who need us to be brave, to take those steps. Had I not decided to move forward, I may have been safe, but I am almost certain I would not have been nearly as successful.

I was hurting, I was crying, yet I kept walking. I would not be stopped, even though I wanted to give up. Eventually, a man whom I later discovered went by the name "Big Phil from the Rim Shop," pulled up in a black Cadillac Escalade to ask if I needed help. I felt stupid, because I knew that this was how most stories of abduction begin, but I was desperate. I needed to get to that store. He told me that I wasn't that far and he would be happy to give me a lift. I prayed and accepted his offer for help, relieved to sit down, if only for a few moments. We pulled up, and the store was closed. I was devastated and I broke down, but my new friend calmed me, pulled out his cell and began dialing a number.

He made a phone call, and within minutes the lights were on and the door was unlocked for me to enter. As I wiped my tears, I walked in and started approaching two men in their late 20s who were clearly in charge, the feeling was surreal. I told them about my desire to work for them and my journey getting there. A few minutes later, I was offered a job on the spot. I was finally in the entertainment business.

Wu Wear was an intimate environment. I worked retail, selling merchandise and interacting with customers and fans on the ground level. Although it was a very casual environment, I was still expected to be on time and accountable. Wu

Wear was a place of business, and I was expected to treat it as such. The more I proved myself, the more responsibility was added to my plate. I started working campus promotions and did event planning for the group. I also picked them up from the airport. Ghostface Killah, Ol' Dirty Bastard and other Wu-Tang Clan group members would pile into my '95 Toyota Camry that my parents finally allowed me to bring down to Atlanta, and I would take them wherever they needed to go.

I quickly developed a thick skin working around them. They were blunt, and when I made mistakes they were quick to let me know. I was on the lowest rung of the ladder of success, but I focused on the fact that I was at least on the ladder. I envisioned myself on the other side of this opportunity, successful and walking in my purpose. I never thought, not even for a moment, that I would stagnate. However, I was willing to be there, be present and do what I needed to do to get to the next level, but within the boundaries that I'd set for myself and that were instilled in me back home.

At Clark Atlanta, I began forming friendships with like-minded students who were also interested in the entertainment business. There was no real rhyme or reason to our becoming close.

We just realized that we had similar goals, and wanted to push one another to attain them. Treat everyone kindly, because you never know the greatness that lies ahead of them in the future. We would sit in our dorm rooms and common areas, surrounded by generic furniture made with cheap fabric and wood, and talk about hip-hop and what made it relevant. We talked about race, sexism and colorism. Those late night conversations about life, that sometimes lasted until dawn, were where we found our commonality. Many of my friends from those days, who were virtually unknown at the time, went on to become quite successful, such as DJ Drama, Bryan-Michael Cox, Bobby Valentino, Polow da Don, Damien Lemon and Mase. I majored in Political Science, but wasn't active in SGA or any pre-law organizations. I thought that I could possibly become an entertainment lawyer, but my focus was definitely more on entertainment than law.

Clark was a special place. There was an energy there that motivated and inspired greatness. I believe, had I been anywhere else, the aspirations my friends and I had would have been seen as pipe dreams, but at Clark, they were attainable goals. We were learning to trust our gut and allowed the voice inside of us to lead and grow louder, drowning out any negativity. We were focused, but we also worked hard and, at times, played harder.

Celebrities and entertainers must have felt this energy as well. It was commonplace to see Jay-Z sitting on the steps of our library or Usher driving through campus. On my way to class one day, a guy in his 20s approached me and asked if I wanted to be in a music video. He gave very little detail and I could tell he was used to girls just saying *yes*. Whether it was because I was a naturally shy person or because it just seemed a little sketchy, something didn't feel right. I politely turned him down and continued walking to class. When the music video for "My Baby Daddy" by hip-hop group B-Rock and the Bizz debuted on BET and I recognized many of my classmates in the video, I silently chuckled. The song was a smash hit, but the lyrics and the video were embarrassing to say the least. The people I knew who participated cringe about it to this day. YouTube is not their friend.

For some reason, I never wanted to be the girl in the video. I always wanted to be the girl behind the lens, making the decisions, establishing the creative direction and driving the business. This is no slight to those who have chosen to do music videos – many of them are my friends, but I knew at an early age that I wanted more longevity and frankly, more power, and that it wasn't for me.

During summer breaks from college, I split my time and worked for the Upward Bound program as a youth counselor. The organization gives under-privileged and at-risk high school students the tools and opportunity to go to college. Although I wasn't labeled at-risk while in high school, I did know how it felt to almost miss the opportunity to go to college. Now that I was enjoying that experience, I wanted to make sure that every young person who had a desire to further their education had the opportunity. I felt a real connection with my students. It didn't feel like work. I got to see how I made a difference in my community, one student at a time. One young lady who stood out in the program was Shera Everette. Shera was different. She didn't care about clothes, hair or what was hot at the time, but instead she had a passion for working in the WNBA. She and I bonded immediately and I became her mentor. She had hopes and dreams that were different and she had a drive and passion that I knew would endure. Shera went on to accomplish many of her dreams and has now become an outstanding professional woman. We keep in touch to this day. Through that experience, I learned that while I was helping the students, those summers also helped me. They helped me to see the power of young people and the difference we can make in the world around us. It was critical that I learned and understood this power firsthand. It would serve me well in the years to come.

At the end of those summer breaks, I always looked forward to returning to Atlanta. It was a fun city with a vibrant nightlife. The student body focused more on the social happenings of the city than any kind of sporting events. While some of my classmates saw going out solely as an opportunity to let loose and enjoy themselves, I saw it as business. Being in the center of the urban music industry, I never knew who would show up at a club or an event. Moreover, I never knew who could potentially be watching me, and I wanted to make sure I was always at my best.

One night, at Club 112, a group of friends and I were having fun when Toni Braxton entered the room. The room stopped and all eyes were fixated on her. Except mine. While Toni's beauty was breathtaking and her star power was undeniable, my eyes were focused on the tiny, powerful young woman walking alongside her in baggy jeans and a t-shirt – Shanti Das. Shanti was the industry executive behind the Toni Braxton brand. Toni had the talent, but Shanti had the power. That night, I studied her as she quietly and calmly controlled the room. This compact little lady was clearly in charge as she handled Toni that evening like a pro and controlled the environment her artist was in like a seasoned vet. She had no idea who I was. Didn't even look in my direction. But I decided that one day she would become my mentor. It took almost a decade, but that's exactly what happened.

As I progressed in college, I started to become popular. I went from working exclusively in retail at Wu Wear to handling their campus promotions. They knew that I took the responsibilities of my job seriously, and that I had a pulse on one of their target audiences. Anticipating the needs and trends of college students was a marketing goldmine in the industry. People on campus and around Atlanta started to recognize my name.

I was dating someone when all of this started happening, and he did not want me to be a part of it. He wanted to be the gatekeeper to my success and didn't like me in the company of powerful men. At the time, I was blinded to the amount of control and manipulation he had over my life. He was older, drove a nice car and hung out with people that, until we got together, I'd only seen on television and read about in magazines. He was not afraid to use his money and influence to get what he wanted. One night, he picked me up from Wu Wear and asked me to quit my job. I thought he was kidding. Then, he offered to give me double the amount of money I was making to leave. As a struggling college student, money is tantalizing and obvious bait. The money was tempting – very tempting, but I declined.

That evening was a defining moment in my life. I realized that passion does not have a price tag. I was confronted with a test of my values. Did I believe in what I was doing? Did I really think that my hard work would pay off in the end? I was a broke college student who worked part-time making very little money. I liked nice clothes and going out. And I could seemingly have had far more financially by dating him, than by working hard. However, in turning him down, I let him know and reminded myself of something much more valuable

– that my dreams were not, are not, and will never be for sale.

Being a young woman in that environment and being able to stand out in a way that is positive can bring out a myriad of insecurities. I often wondered if I was pretty enough or smart enough. I wondered if my hair was long enough or my clothes expensive enough. At the time, my style was what I referred to as "pretty tomboy." My clothing choices were inspired by TLC, and I was a sneakerhead. Still am. But I also liked to dress up, and play with different hairstyles. I went back and forth between short hair and weave, red and blonde hair. Between my junior and senior year of college, I started incorporating designer labels into my wardrobe. You'll find that most Historically Black College and University (HBCU) campuses are like fashion shows, and Clark was no exception. Every penny that I made regretfully went into my appearance and wardrobe, a worthy but unwise investment. Finding a style that fit my personality helped to establish my individuality and quiet some of the insecurities that plagued my mind. I was starting to *build my brand.*

I wondered if being me would be enough to achieve these over-the-top goals I had set for myself. I honestly felt myself shrink sometimes in those rooms, as all those insecurities seemed to hit me at the very moment I needed to stand tall. As a woman, I quickly tired of being compared to other women. I saw that other women were dealing with many of the same issues, and it seemed that the more put together and attractive the woman was on the outside, the more she battled with self-esteem issues internally.

I really started to notice this once I began participating in fashion shows on and off campus. Not only did others start equating how I looked to who I was, I somewhat bought into it as well. Some people only liked me because they thought I was "pretty," but others hated me for the same reason. The more I started to gain confidence and come out of my shell, the more negativity seemed to come my way. One girl, whom I'd never met before and didn't attend Clark, came to my dorm one evening determined to fight me. She never said I did anything to her. I just offended her by being me. She yelled and cursed for me to come out and fight her for what seemed like hours, and I could not understand what I'd done wrong. She eventually left, but that incident stayed with me. In time, I came to realize that people often try to find external scapegoats for their internal battles. This is why introspection and self-reflection is so vital to our growth. We have to see ourselves for who we are if we are to move forward.

CHAPTER FOUR

The Cost Of Success

"If you continuously compete with others, you become bitter.
But if you continuously compete with yourself, you become better."

— Unknown

So many women fall victim to their insecurities. They stop focusing on their end-goal, preferring to linger in whatever is in front of them at the moment. They feel that there is an infinite amount of time to address the things that hold them back, but there isn't. Tomorrow is not promised, and when we become aware that there are obstacles we need to overcome, no matter how large or small, we must become proactive in tackling them so we can move forward. Most times, we get off track because we are afraid to confront our weaknesses, and even more afraid to acknowledge them. We procrastinate, hoping to avoid what we know is there, but when we do that, our problems loom larger and threaten to overtake us.

By the end of my junior year, I was offered the job of executive assistant at Mike Tyson Enterprises. Mike was the heavyweight champion of the world and his business manager was my mentor, Shawnee Simms. Shawnee was a powerhouse in the boxing industry and as the muscle behind one of the most powerful and feared men in the world, her business savvy was impeccable. She exposed me to the world of private jets, Lamborghini's and homes in gated communities, but most importantly, she taught me the art of doing business as a woman in a male-dominated industry. Shawnee's negotiating skills were shrewd and she never accepted 'no' as an answer to anything. The biggest lesson I learned was that when, as a woman, in a standoff during negotiations, the first person to make the next move – never wins. It exposes their weaknesses. She was right.

My insecurities led me to a crossroads in my senior year. I knew I wanted to work in entertainment, but my degree in Political Science, and the roadmap set by my parents dictated that law school would be the safer choice. After my lackluster performance in high school, I had to be certain that I would not fail. I could not disappoint my parents. I had it made. At 22 years-old, before even obtaining my degree, I had my foot in the door of the entertainment industry. I sat ringside at fights in Las Vegas. I was coordinating matches at Caesar's Palace. Mike Tyson and Shawnee personally attended my college graduation. The doors were open to me. Opportunity was beckoning me to enter. Out of fear, I resigned from Mike Tyson Enterprises soon after graduation.

How has fear held you back from pursuing your dream?

_____

_____

_____

_____

_____

_____

_____

Instead of coordinating physical fights, I began working in the political boxing ring for the re-election campaign of Chief Justice Henry Frye back in North Carolina. I worked as his field coordinator. Our campaign staff worked our butts off and my job was to register people to vote and get them to the polls on Election Day. Our candidate was well respected and the incumbent. Everyone expected him to be a shoo-in, but we didn't take it for granted. We knew that having a Democratic African-American man in a statewide office in North Carolina was a bit of an anomaly. North Carolina was always a traditionally Republican state, and we were still creating opportunities for more diverse representation that accurately reflected the racial and gender demographics. Even in the new millennium, after integration and the Voting Rights Act were enacted, we were still actively pursuing a breakthrough in our local and state government. I knew from growing up with a father who championed civil rights in his career and life that it was important that we have representatives who can identify with us and make certain our voices are heard.

We were always on the move. I must have driven across the state at least twenty times during the course of the campaign. Many times during those long road trips, Chief Justice Frye would talk to me about service and about our duty to help underserved communities. Our communities were crying out for support, and we had to use our talents, skills, and education to provide it. I felt that

I was doing something important, that my work mattered and made a difference in people's lives.

When Election Day came, we gathered for a victory party that ended far less than victorious. We lost. We were beat out by a young attorney and I sobbed with disappointment. The next morning, I began to evaluate where we went wrong. While we out-raised the opposition, we could have done a better job of investing in young people and meeting them where they were – on colleges campuses, at social gatherings and on the web. We used traditional campaign methods and did not expand our reach.

My stomach turned as I studied for the LSAT. Everything about my decision felt wrong. Motivated almost entirely by fear, I entered North Carolina Central University School of Law, my parents' alma mater, to begin the next part of my journey. The very school I was reluctant to attend as a senior in high school, would now be my academic home for the next three years as a law student. I had officially accepted my fate. At the cusp of a breakthrough that comes with graduation and making concrete decisions about the route my life would take, I chose to play it safe instead of moving forward.

Honestly, I had no idea what *moving forward* looked like. I had worked as a grunt woman at the bottom rung of the entertainment industry while in school, left a great paying job in the boxing industry and quit instead of climbing higher. So often, we don't even realize how very close we are to reaching a greater level of success when we give up. We have to live knowing that we didn't do what we truly wanted, and are now living on someone else's terms instead of our own.

CHAPTER FIVE

Stand Down

"Great work is done by people who are not afraid to be great."

– Fernando Flores

Fear is a nasty disease and, if you let it, will completely change the course of your life. In law school, I was physically present each day, but my mind was totally absent. I was under a microscope. Everyone knew who I was. I could not get away with blowing off a class. If I even seemed to be slacking off, a professor would call to check on me. The faculty was focused on making sure I did not tarnish the legacy that my parents paved. So, I showed up. I did enough to keep everyone off my back. Yet, rather than studying civil procedure, I continued to study the music business. I watched as the students around me were engrossed in torts and case studies, excited about their futures as attorneys. They were intense and passionate about the law. With a level of intensity and almost desperation that I had never experienced before, I learned everything there was to know about the entertainment business.

I knew that my next move would determine the rest of my life.

Each day, I would sit in class and surf the web looking for inspiration from women who paved the way. As I researched the biographies of my modern day sheroes, Oprah Winfrey, Sylvia Rhone, Debra Lee and Cathy Hughes, I couldn't seem to find the bridge from where they started to the point when they actually "made it." Where were the stories that shared where I was on my journey? Where was the blueprint and that missing link? When did they crumble and fall apart, and how did they pick up the pieces?

I desperately needed that guidance at the time, because I too was personally falling apart. My spirit was broken, my face had broken out into hives and I was waking up each day feeling like I was in the wrong place. I was being taught the wrong things. I was surrounded by people who were equally determined and equally passionate, but with a completely different agenda than anything that fit where I was supposed to be. I was *living a lie*. My apartment was a lie. My classes were a lie. My studies were a lie. Nothing about law school resonated in my spirit as *my truth*.

While I love my parents and while we are cut from the same cloth – *we are not the same.* My entire life I was playing a game of make-pretend. Pretending to think like them, pretending to enjoy the things that they enjoyed and pretending to want to be an attorney knowing all along this was the farthest thing from the truth. While sitting in law school as a 1L, or first year law student, during my spring semester, it hit me like a ton of bricks. It was time for me to start thinking like an adult and to get in the driver's seat of my own life, but I didn't know where to begin. So, I began to write a mission statement.

> **Mission statement:** To become the head of an entertainment company that will transform lives with a laser focus on helping women and girls.

When I wrote my mission statement, I was 23-years old and had no idea what it truly meant and if it were even attainable. All I knew when writing it was that it came from the purest place of my head and heart, and it felt very real. For me, I needed this creed to help shape my goals and to order my next steps.

Take a moment now to really think about your life's mission and attempt to get it down to one or two sentences. Take away, even if for just a moment, your fears and other people's expectations of you, and write from a clear space.

Your mission statement:

_____

_____

_____

_____

_____

From the moment I wrote my mission statement to this day, I have referenced it in almost every decision I've ever made in life. Once you declare to yourself and to the world your purpose, the universe begins to align all the tools required for you to make those dreams happen. The first major decision I made, once I had a clear mission statement, was to quit law school. I didn't broadcast my decision to the world; instead, I told only a select group of people. The ones who had firsthand knowledge of the internal struggle I had faced over that year, were supportive. The people who had always followed a more traditional set of standards did not support me. However, law school did not align with my mission. I knew what I had to do.

I completed my first year of law school, and took out a student loan knowing that I would not return. I told my parents an untruth. As I ended the lease to my apartment without their knowledge, I told them I would be traveling to New York City to work as a clerk in a law firm for the summer. They reluctantly agreed, but deep down they knew the story didn't add up. I didn't want them to worry about me. It didn't matter. They were plenty worried. They felt that I was throwing away a secure future to chase after an idea in a city known for ripping people and their souls to the core. They wished me the best, but also told me that they could not financially support my decision. If I was going to make it, I'd have to do it *on my own.*

I know I didn't go about it the right way. I wasn't ready to stand boldly in my truth. I had really *just* accepted it in my spirit. When you find an opportunity to exit from the wrong path in order to re-route to the right one, you have to seize it. However, there is a better way to accomplish the transition other than breaking trust. I wish I had known that at the time. I encourage you to be forthright and honest in declaring the path that accompanies your purpose. Nevertheless, I accepted the challenge given by my parents and headed to New York City.

Do you need to re-route your path? How can you make that happen while maintaining integrity?

_____

_____

_____

_____

_____

_____

_____

Your calling requires special people and unique change-agents in your life to bring it to fruition. My best friend, Sabrina, is one of those people. I packed my bags with my student loan money in tow and crashed on Sabrina's couch in the Crown Heights area of Brooklyn. This was before the now sexy Brooklyn; the Brooklyn now known as the home of the Brooklyn Nets. But this was a time when parts of Brooklyn were known as "Do or Die Bed-Stuy." I took heed.

The closet I lived in, in the dead of summer, had no air conditioning and there was barely enough room for me to stretch my legs, but it was there that I felt complete happiness and freedom for the first time in my adult life. As I entered the bustling streets of New York City and traveled on the subway, I had no concrete plan, but I knew it was there that I would find my calling.

Each day, I interviewed for unpaid internships with any potential employer that could get me closer to my dreams. After weeks of applying online, I received an email from Arista Records requesting that I come in for an interview. While the position was unpaid, I felt this could be my big break. They represented Sean "Diddy" Combs, Whitney Houston, Outkast and some of the biggest names in the business.

As I entered their office, I was completely in awe of all of the platinum plaques on the walls, yet I felt out of place. Dressed in a dark business suit, fake pearls and my hair tied in a bun, the staffer in charge of the interview sat across from me in ripped jeans and a t-shirt and began the interview.

"Sooooo, what makes you want to work for Arista Records?"

"This job will give *me* an opportunity to advance *my* goal to work in the music business."

"I see you are in law school, why do you want to work in the music business?"

"*My* dream is to become the head of an entertainment company and this position will give *me* a great start."

Everything I said and offered to them, however, *was all about me.* I hit all the wrong notes. After rambling on for ten minutes and sticking to my pre-rehearsed script, I could see his eyes glaze over as he abruptly dismissed me from his office. Devastated, I couldn't understand why no one would hire me – not even to work for *free.* I needed to figure something out quickly, or I would have to go home and back to a life I didn't want for myself.

"To be yourself in a world that is constantly trying to make you something else is the greatest accomplishment."

– Ralph Waldo Emerson

When I looked in the mirror after that interview, I didn't even recognize myself. How can I, a so-called hip-hop head, walk into a meeting at a record label in a suit and pearls? Not only was I not properly representing the culture I so desperately wanted to be a part of, I wasn't even accurately representing myself. I've never been a suit kind of girl. I was more of the girl who would rock jeans, killer heels and a cute shirt. My hair was never in a bun – ever. Instead, I switched between flowing locks and a short cut. That was it, I had become a programmed and conditioned robot and I had to break the mold.

For me, that was a defining moment. While intelligence and what talents you bring to the table are key, your personal brand and how well you will fit into corporate culture *does matter*. Most importantly, you want to start a job the way you will finish. If you're more into wearing your hair natural or your style is more business casual, interview as the real you and not your *representative.*

Job interviews are like dating. You never [or shouldn't] marry the first boy you meet and you may have to kiss a few frogs before you meet your prince, so shop around, explore and try to embrace the painful process.

One of the most important things I learned within that process was that companies were only interested in how I could add value to their brand. Although they needed to know and understand my goals, they did not care about what *I thought they could do for me.* They already knew what they could do for me. These companies had employed hundreds, if not thousands, of young college graduates and witnessed their success and failure within their ranks before I ever came in to interview with them. They knew the open positions and the phone calls they could make to put my career in orbit. My only job during the interview was to let them know how I could be of use to *them.* I was so busy telling interviewers about my five-year plan and complete backstory that I forgot to tell them what I bring to the table. If you have had issues in landing a job or closing a deal, take a different approach. Your sole goal during the interview is to show how you will *add immediate value* to their company and bottom line.

5 Tenets for Rocking the Interview

1. Exude confidence. Make direct eye contact, have a firm handshake, and stand straight. Be aware of your power, but don't be arrogant. You don't own the position yet, but you have what it takes to earn it.

2. Highlight your strengths, but be willing to acknowledge areas of weakness. Illustrate how your strengths will add value to the company, and the proactive methods you will use to make sure your weaknesses are not a liability.

3. Clearly communicate how you define success as it relates to your work and your plan to make an immediate impact, if hired. Let the potential employer also know how you will measure success if offered the position.

4. Have fun and be yourself. Maintain a professional demeanor, but don't be afraid to let your potential employer see who you really are.

5. Don't take it personal if you don't get the position. Be gracious, sincerely thanking the employer for the opportunity to interview. You were able to get more comfortable with the process, and your gracious attitude may make them think of you should another position open up.

"As an intern, you are a liability.
It's your job to prove you are an asset."

– Kevin Liles

As I was figuring out the basic tenets of rocking an interview, I was spotted by a casting director for ABC one day on the train and I ended up auditioning for the now-defunct soap opera All My Children as an extra, and got the gig. They invited me back, and soon I became a regular extra, and was making regular money. I moved off of Sabrina's couch and into an apartment with my friend Kristi Henderson. Acting wasn't quite what I wanted to do, but it was exciting, I was working in entertainment and making money, so I pushed myself to be content. From learning lines to daily glam sessions and sharing scenes with major stars like Susan Lucci, everything was moving along until January 2001, when I was let go. I knew that pilot season was starting in LA, and there were casting calls everywhere, so I went out there to audition. I got very close on a few different projects, but could never secure a role. I enrolled in acting school, hoping it would help me perfect my "craft," but instead, I discovered through that process that I was not an actress. Each day in class, it didn't feel natural. As an aspiring actress, I wasn't horrible, but I was average at-best and knew that whatever I chose to do professionally, I wanted to be exceptional at it.

"Whatever you are, be a good one."

– Abraham Lincoln

Where do you shine? Are you pursuing a career that showcases your talent?

_____

_____
_____
_____
_____
_____
_____

Not only were we not born to be average, we were born to be the very best. We were designed and crafted for a very specific purpose on this earth and it is our job to discover and master it. The contribution we give to this planet is the debt we owe for the life we live. We cannot afford to squander our talents nor waste opportunities. We were created for that purpose and it is our responsibility to fulfill it.

In my heart, I always knew I wasn't an actress. However, when that opportunity, which seemingly aligned with my mission statement, landed in my lap with very little effort, I thought that I could possibly take it farther than it was ever meant to go. That role was a means to an end. It gave me what I needed at the time, which was experience in some form of the entertainment industry and money. However, it did not highlight my unique talents and skills. I'm glad I was aware, alert and in tune enough to realize this was not my path. I needed to go back to square one and find a job or internship that could really take me where I needed to be.

CHAPTER SIX

Coldest Winter Ever

"Personal relationships are always the key to good business."
– Lindsay Fox

The winter of 2002 was brutal in New York City. Although I knew I had made the right decision in coming back to the East Coast to pursue my passion for the business of entertainment, the icy winds and snowy streets tore through my skin and seeped into my doubts.

After sending my resume to hundreds of potential employers, I faced the harsh reality that something had to change – and fast. One day, I fell asleep at the computer screen after an all day marathon of posting my resume online. I felt inadequate, small and like a complete failure. Where had I gone wrong? What was I not doing right? Surely, finding a job with a college degree can't be this difficult, or can it?

Now, I believe that technology and social media are wonderful tools to utilize in creating your brand and engaging your audience, however, nothing beats a phone call or conversation to get to the next level professionally. I've never received a job or any meaningful career opportunity through online resume submissions. That's why it is extremely important to network, and to make sure that you are always bringing the best possible *you* to the table. I am sure that *someone* has gotten a job through filling out an online application, but most people I know have not. Most people get jobs because someone recognizes a strength or passion in them that would be a perfect fit for a person or company they know. Every job I've had is because of a conversation that occurred on my behalf, or that I initiated.

Building relationships is vital to success. Relationships are built by speaking to one another, sharing the same space, and spending one-on-one time. Strong foundations are formed when you stop bombarding people with what *you* want, and allow them to *experience* you. You are more than your business card. You are deeper than your online profile, and you are far more prolific than your blog. Show people who you are, and remind them of this after you part ways. Invite them to coffee to learn more about them. Send flowers and handwritten thank you notes to show that you appreciate them taking time out of their schedules to spend with you. Doing these things creates a far more lasting impression than hitting "send" on your online resume. Creating an opportunity to show people who you are is a surefire way to garner success.

That's exactly what I did. After submitting my resume online for positions at The Gersh Agency, a small boutique talent agency that represents actors, I began a new follow-up strategy. I began calling the company once a day, at the same time every day, at 11 a.m. When that didn't work, I visited the company and staked (stalked) out their lobby for any possible sighting of a Gersh employee. Finally, a young man, at the bottom of the ladder decided to bring me on-board. It was unpaid, and I had no money. Still, I decided to take on the internship as if I expected to run the company one day. I came in early and left late. I ran errands, got coffee, and did all the things that the employees either did not want or did not have the time to do. It was hard work. There was no paycheck to be received on Fridays. I felt invisible. They filed all of the interns in a back office and we were expected to only be seen and not heard.

I had rent to pay. I needed to eat. I felt like I was taking a step forward in my career, but I was struggling financially. I knew that I could take a full-time job outside of the entertainment industry, but doing so would come at the expense of my dream. I decided that the dream was worth the struggle and I got odd jobs to support myself. I was a telemarketer. I was a waitress. People were hanging up on me, cussing me out, being pigs and leaving no tips, and treating me as if I were less than a person. Just a few months before, I was on a television show. It was very humbling to know that circumstances can change so quickly. Back home in NC, everyone was still so excited I had been rubbing elbows with Susan Lucci, and thought I had major deals in the pipeline as an actress. As far as they were concerned, I had *made it* in New York City. Honestly, I was too ashamed to tell them otherwise. I didn't want anyone judging me, thinking that I made a terrible decision by chasing some crazy dream when I could have been pursuing a perfectly acceptable career as an attorney. Now, I'm proud that I made the tough decision to stick it out, and start from the very bottom to get what I wanted. There is no shame in doing what it takes to finance your dream. I did honest work, and I made honest pay. I was running my business as my grandmother taught me, and I should not have cared how people were running their mouths. They weren't paying my rent.

Eventually, someone did notice me. He noticed my work ethic for a job that provided nothing more than an opportunity, and he was impressed. He also happened to be one of the senior agents at the company. One day, he called me into his office.

"Why are you here? And why do you work so hard unpaid?"

I explained to him my passion for the entertainment business and my complete dedication to my purpose. Through our brief conversation, I shared with him that I worked previously for Mike Tyson Enterprises, but quit my dream job out of fear and entered law school. My transparency was received well. While I sat there, he called one of his friends who worked for HBO Sports and scheduled an interview for me.

CHAPTER SEVEN

The New Slave

"Your network is your net worth"

– Porter Gale

After five extremely long and grueling interviews, I was hired at HBO Boxing as the Executive Assistant to the Vice President. I finally had my foot in the door. Who knew a complete stranger would create an opportunity for me that would align me right back in an area where I'd given up – boxing? I had a paid position, with benefits. There was potential room for advancement. My parents could breathe and tell everyone that I was gainfully employed. I was officially a badge-carrying member of corporate America. By all accounts, I had worked for this exact moment. I was able to marry the entertainment component I desired with the traditional, corporate stability that allowed my parents to stop having nightmares about me being homeless and hungry in New York. Yet, something still did not feel quite right.

My first day on the job my boss was fired. There were allegations of misconduct, and I felt very uneasy. Still, I persisted because this job allowed me to feel something that I had previously lacked—financial comfort. I could pay my bills. I could buy some clothes. I could go out to dinner without having to look to my gainfully employed friends to take care of the check. Financial comfort has the ability to lull a person into complacency. I knew it could be worse. I knew that New York could toss me around like litter and force me back to my small North Carolina town, completely hopeless and totally defeated. I knew I could have remained stuck in law school, with nerve and anxiety issues, a face full of acne, and still broke. I did not want that to be my story. I did not want to be that loser. So, even though I didn't quite fit into corporate America, I stayed. Yet, I continuously asked God and myself what I was missing.

"Make your passion your paycheck."
– Nicole Williams

While at work one day, I saw Russell Simmons on television. He was talking about President Bill Clinton. Simmons stressed that young people would be the determining factor in future elections, and politicians had to find avenues to reach them. One of those avenues was through music and entertainment. The talking heads and pundits on the television and radio shows, which featured political roundtables, were not relatable to young people. They saw them as old and boring, and subsequently, tuned them out.

Watching that segment lit a fire in me. In Russell Simmons, I saw how politics and entertainment could work in tandem. I knew in that moment that the piece I felt was missing actually existed. This was something attainable that people were talking about, and more importantly, doing, all while I sat in financial corporate comfort. I knew I had to make a move. There was no time to procrastinate. If I felt this way, certainly others did as well, and I needed to create an opportunity. Not moving forward on this thing that I could not fully articulate, yet resonated in my spirit would have almost ensured that I would not find meaning, passion, and purpose in my work. So, I took advantage of my current position.

"Let your day job finance your passion"

– Valeisha Butterfield Jones

Most of us do not have the luxury of leaving a paid position to chase our dreams. In my case, I certainly did not, so rather than making the spontaneous decision to leave, I launched into full investigative mode. Although I wasn't crazy about my corporate job, it placed me exactly where I needed to be – in the company of very smart, well-connected people. As I began forming relationships within the company, I started casually inquiring about Russell Simmons. After several months, an assistant within the company slipped me his personal email address over lunch one day. As I sat there staring at Russell Simmons' email address, I started preparing to make my next move.

In order to succeed, you eventually have to take a leap of faith. Depending on your stage of life, that leap will take different forms. In my early twenties, with no one depending on me and little overhead, I could afford to take huge risks because I didn't have a lot to lose. I hadn't acquired anything yet. However, I think it's a mistake and disservice to your passion and talent to let age and obligations hinder you from pursuing your dreams. You are worthy of that leap. It may have to be more calculated. You may have to work out every detail to ensure that you meet your obligations. But, prepare, and then take that leap.

There's a huge difference between preparation and procrastination. Procrastination breeds excuses. Things always hinder you from achieving your goal. Every little thing becomes an insurmountable obstacle, leaving you with no energy whatsoever to tackle the actual tribulations that will inevitably arise. On the other hand, preparation is daily, even hourly research in order to procure a desired result. I held on to that email address for a good while, until I had a well-thought-out plan of attack in place. I wanted to work for Russell Simmons. I wanted to be a part of the future of entertainment and politics in any way I could. I not only studied his story, but also his habits. I considered the fact that he self-diagnosed himself as having Attention Deficit Disorder (ADD) when I crafted my email. I knew it had to be short, sweet and to the point. I also knew that I had to send it very early in the morning if I had any chance of him reading it because through my online research, he woke up each morning at 5 a.m. to meditate. I only had one shot at getting this right. I also said a prayer. I prayed for God to order my steps, to guide my words and I also prayed that my intentions for working in the entertainment business remained good.

Mr. Simmons,

My name is Valeisha Butterfield. I dropped out of law school against my parents' wishes to move to New York City. My dream is to work in the entertainment industry and to give back to my community. I am contacting you to first thank you for being a strong blueprint and to add value to your company. I'm willing to start at the bottom and will do whatever it takes to prove that having me on-board will be a decision you won't regret. Thank you for your time.

Yours in service,
Valeisha

Russell Simmons, a man who receives thousands of emails each week, responded to my random, unsolicited email within five minutes. He asked me to schedule a meeting with his assistant. I sent a message to his assistant right away. However, it took over a month for her to respond. The high I initially felt had waned into worry and impatience. Why was she taking so long? Didn't she know she was messing with my life? I was ready to work, but was stuck at my job until I got the green light from the assistant. It was one of my first realizations of the extraordinary power that gatekeepers possess. They choose whether to unlock the door or not, and they choose when. I did not bombard her with emails, but I persisted in asking for a meeting. After all, Russell Simmons said he wanted to meet with me!

"Patience is passion tamed."

– Lyman Abbott

However, I refused to be anything other than professional and kind, because my reaction to the delay was essential in making sure this meeting actually took place. We often get so impatient and so pushy when things don't go according to our plans. It can bring out the worst in us. We're thinking of our issues, our agenda, our dilemmas, our troubles, with little or no regard to what is happening on the other side of a perceived chance or opportunity. My email stated that I wanted to add value to Russell Simmons' company. I told him briefly about who I was and what I'd gone through to get to the place that allowed his email address to find its way to me (or for me to be able to dig for it). If I was truly going to do whatever it took, then I had to do perhaps the most difficult thing there is – wait. We must have faith in God's timing, especially when it's scary. We must have faith in the process. She did eventually respond and scheduled an appointment for the next month. I was definitely acquiring patience.

On the day of my appointment with Russell Simmons, I did my hair. I put on my make-up. I did not look like a supermodel. I looked like me. I looked like what I was – a working, but seemingly broke, struggling, recent college graduate trying to succeed in New York City. I was intimidated before I even walked through the doors of the office. The company was on the 43rd floor. The doors were large and heavy, not just in weight, but in power, in promise, and in the standard of excellence that lay within. Once I opened the door, I was taken in by the sheer glamour of the office – the gold-plated lobby, the oversized pictures of the *Phat Farm* and *Baby Phat* brands, the life-size pictures of Kimora and their kids. There were password-protected doors and even a 300-lb security guard. I felt like I was experiencing a scene from a dream. I sat there for almost thirty minutes taking everything in.

I walked through the inner office doors and sat across from Russell. There was no security and no entourage. There was just the two of us – me, with big dreams, and him, with the power to make those dreams a reality. I started to speak, wanting to introduce myself, but before I could, he said:

"Who are you, and what the fuck are you doing in my office?"

Oh. My. God. Every crazy thought I'd ever had came flooding in. My first instinct was to fake a heart attack, drop to the floor and let a stretcher carry me away, back into my stable job and predictable life. But there was a voice, nagging and screaming inside of me.

"This is the moment you've been waiting for! You got this! Now own it!"

I had two choices – shrink or grow. Even though I physically wanted to shrink (or faint), I decided to grow. I decided to take the chance on my future and myself.

"I was called to serve, and that is why I am here. I just want an opportunity."

A few minutes later, he introduced me to the entire staff as the new slave. I had accepted the position. I was an intern, again. I was unpaid, again. My parents had nightmares about my impending hunger and homelessness, again. Though it seemed from outside appearances that I had taken a step backwards, I knew that I had just embarked on a journey that would forever change the trajectory of my life. Now, I only needed to heed the words Russell left me with as he walked out that first day.

"Put your head down and do the work."

I remained the "slave" of the organization for the next ten months. I handled every shipping request, filed papers, and fetched coffee. I even sat in the office of a Baby Phat executive who was much younger than me, but more experienced, who had a file cabinet overrun with thousands of magazines. He told me to organize each magazine in chronological order while he sat on the phone and smoked cigarettes – for six or more hours. It was grueling, tedious work. However, I was a willing sponge. I learned everything about the structure of the company. I learned who the players were. This was a very valuable lesson for me, because I'd mistakenly believed, prior to this experience, that the players all worked in corner offices and had fancy titles of Director or higher. I thought that their job descriptions were lengthy and their authority absolute. I could not have been more wrong. These people have the YES or NO vote that can signal an entrance or exit within a company, but the real power players are the assistants, the coordinators, and the interns who are the gatekeepers for those with the corner offices. They have the trust of those who hold executive decisions, and are often asked their opinions of people who are seeking entry into the company. People, like Russell's assistant, can make or break you with a few words. I became friends with the gatekeepers. I sought them out in different departments. I treated them as if they were themselves Russell Simmons, because, in a way, they were.

Anytime one builds a company and hires a person to perform a specific task, they are, in essence, duplicating themselves, their values, and their output in order to become more productive. We were all representatives of Russell Simmons' brand, and it was not only important that we showed that with our work, but also with the way we treated people outside of the organization as well as those within it. Unfortunately, there are many people in positions at various companies who have let the power go to their heads without realizing that by simply showing respect to people, it will work to their benefit and to the advancement of their careers. It's more effective to motivate your staff by empowering them, than by tearing them down.

CHAPTER EIGHT

The Breakthrough

*"We are rich only through what we give;
and poor only through what we refuse and keep."*

– Anne Swetchine

I found a sweet spot in the non-profit arm of the organization. Originally, I'd wanted to work on the music side, but because of my passion for helping others, Russell saw where I could make a real difference. Seeing my willingness and desire to serve, he re-directed me from where I wanted to be, to where I needed to be. I worked on the development of financial literacy programs that served at-risk communities, but incorporated celebrities and entertainment elements into each of my project plans. My first event took place in Detroit, Michigan. It was an event completely engineered by me and executed by the team I had put together. It was show time and car services began to arrive with Eminem, Common and other special guests we'd invited in tow. The room was full of thousands of young people eager to see their favorite stars and learn about budgeting their money. The mood was set and as the panelists stood for a group photo at the end of the program, Russell grabbed the microphone and asked me to come to the stage. He wanted me to be recognized for my hard work. He wanted me to be in that group photo. He wanted me to understand my worth. I played it cool, but deep down I felt complete.

My purpose was validated through my work. I was 100% fulfilled, and never dreaded coming into the office. I was clearly in my zone – being able to combine working in the sexy, pop culture of entertainment while doing work that gave back to the community.

Interestingly, I was learning about financial literacy along with the thousands of people who came out for our *Get Your Money Right* tour. I was starting to make good money, and I was spending it as quickly as I made it. I'd always said that when I started earning a six-figure salary I would have it made. That was my goal. However, when I finally reached those ranks, I wanted to have all the trappings that came along with it. I moved to a nicer apartment. I bought nicer clothes and went on nicer trips. I wanted to keep up with the lifestyle that was around me, and doing that ensured that I still lived paycheck to paycheck despite the increase in salary. So, I decided to take some of the principles that I promoted across the nation and apply it to my own life.

Five Tenets of Financial Literacy

1. Budgeting. Keep an accurate account of all of your expenses. Figure out where you may be wasting money, and research ways to decrease your overhead. If there is more money being paid out than coming in, you either have to make more money to maintain your lifestyle, or downsize your lifestyle to make it fit your money.

2. Saving. It is important to save money for both the short-term and the long-term. Your short-term savings allows for emergencies, job loss, and other surprises that happen in life. Your long-term savings is for retirement. That's the money that will work for you when you become too old to work for it.

3. Investing. Not only should you be saving money, you should be finding ways to grow

your money. By working with a financial professional, you can establish a plan that takes some of the earning stress off of you and onto your money.

4. Improving your score. Your credit score not only determines whether or not you can obtain a loan or mortgage, but how much you will be paying back in interest. To avoid paying over-the-top fees, use a free online system to check your credit, then begin clearing up any debts that you may owe.

5. Finding free/frugal fun. If you never allow yourself to have fun under the guise of being financially responsible, then chances are you will not stick to it. You don't have to spend a ton of money to have fun. Think about creating moments instead of buying stuff. Find free festivals, parks, and activities to do. Perhaps you can even challenge your friends to come up with ways to have fun with a spending limit by using coupons, group rates, and ingenuity.

Because I started at the bottom, I was able to see the holes at the top. In any entertainment-based company, 90% of the workforce is creative people.

They are brilliant. They always have an influx of wonderful and challenging ideas. They are the innovators of the company, crossing and expanding boundaries that propel the company forward. A creative mind can be a beautiful trait. However, creative people are not executors of ideas. They don't want to get bogged down in the details. They are not necessarily concerned with how the project is taken from concept to reality; so many times projects with great potential are never actualized. I watched it happen over and over. Extraordinary concepts. No final products. This is especially disheartening when your focus is on non-profit work and projects that can be of service to the community. I realized my niche, my talent was in the execution of the influx of ideas that were captured within our office walls, but never made it to the communities that really needed it. I was promoted to Project Manager.

"Real integrity is doing the right thing, knowing that nobody's going to know whether you did it or not."

– Oprah Winfrey

This job was more than just an opportunity to prove myself; it was an opportunity to become great at something. I knew what it was to be average, so the realization that the same girl who was told that she would not be able to go to college now held a precious chance to leave an indelible mark as part of one of the best-known organizations in America, was not lost upon me. I was grateful and eager to prove myself. I became so indoctrinated with the projects I worked with, that I became indispensable. Within three years I moved up the ladder, from Project Manager to Director of Sponsorship, to the Executive Director of the Hip-Hop Summit Action Network. In the entertainment business, or any business for that matter, people are easily replaced. There are thousands of other people who are trained to do what you do as well as or better than you are. So, you have to bring the Unique Selling Point (USP) of your personal brand to every project you touch. What is that thing that you have that cannot be found in anyone else? Do you honor it enough to consistently bring it to the table?

Throughout my internship with Russell Simmons, I did not simply work hard; I worked

98

crazy. I worked like my next meal, and even my next breath, depended on it. I averaged about three hours of sleep per night, and on those rare occasions when I was able to relax a little, I slept about six hours. I did this, without complaint, for ten months. When I was finally hired, finally earned a salary, a benefits package, and paid vacation, I really felt as if I had made it. The hard work and dedication I put forth as an intern had finally paid off. I could breathe.

However, the reality of my newfound success soon surfaced. My level of responsibility increased dramatically. I found myself collecting tens of thousands of frequent flyer miles because I was on a plane three or four times a week. The sacrifices of my personal life as an intern paled in comparison to the near-death of my contact with the outside world as an employee. On top of that were the additional pressures within the company. Employees who were more credentialed than I was began to feel threatened by my progression and continued success. They were insecure, and instead of working diligently to make themselves more of an asset, they chose to make my job harder in an effort to make me seem less valuable, less essential.

The night before another major event, more than twenty thousand dollars worth of promotional materials was delivered to my office. As usual, the items were placed near my desk. It was near the end of the day and I left to take a quick bathroom break. In less than five minutes, I returned to my office only to find the entire shipment had been removed. After scanning the office and asking everyone what happened, I quickly realized someone, within our own office, had stolen the items. They were event-specific promotional tools, flyers, tickets and brochures, all items that could not be reused. The culprit had no intentions of ever using those materials. They only wanted to sabotage my success.

As you rise within a company, some will embrace it while others will feel threatened. Well, they didn't know my story. Only *I* carried all of the struggles, all the rejections, and all the failures that brought me to this position. Therefore, I was not about to give them the satisfaction of downgrading my career or losing my temper. If I failed, it would be by my own doing, not the sabotage of others. In this case, and there were many others like it, I simply identified the problem, found the best possible solution, which in this case was a costly rush order of new materials, and charged it to the game.

Even as people attempted to sabotage my success, I found advocates that proved to be instrumental in my life. One of my biggest advocates was the highly-esteemed Dr. Benjamin Chavis. Dr. Ben was the CEO and Co-Chairman (along with Russell Simmons) of the Hip Hop Summit Action Network. A long-time crusader for civil rights and the former Executive Director of the NAACP, he had earned titles and accolades, and could easily have taken a back seat to leadership by giving orders instead of showing his staff *how* to be most effective by being an active participant in day-to-day operations. He had no benefit in taking an interest in me. However, he did. He was my guardian angel, showing me the traps and the landmines of the often-treacherous entertainment industry. He could have sought the spotlight, but he pushed me to the front and not only allowed others to see my light, but for me to see it within myself. He is one of a very few leaders who is willing to pass the torch to the next generation and gives them the tools to achieve and surpass their accomplishments. Often, I'd see Dr. Ben making his own copies, his own coffee, filing papers and the like. There were people who could take care of those things for him, and it taught me a very important lesson. Never be too big to do the small jobs. Do whatever you need to do in order to *get the job done.*

I learned not only the ins and outs of my job, but of the jobs around me. I studied my job in order to work harder, smarter and faster. I was determined to show Russell that I was a wise investment, and not a mistake. I didn't eat right. I didn't sleep well. I worked until or after midnight on many, many nights. Because of this, people I had long-admired in the entertainment industry, like Lisa Ellis, Sylvia Rhone, and Shanti Das, who didn't know I existed, began to learn my name. In one instance, I'd sent an email to music executive Lisa Ellis regarding a celebrity for an awards show. She called my office at midnight, not pleased at all and ready to give my voicemail a piece of her mind, but when I answered the phone, she instantly gained respect for me because we were both still in the office, still working like mad to get our work done.

What I began to learn was that there are very few people who are actually willing to do the work. They want the results, but will not put in the effort. They are willing to work when everyone is watching, but they shut down immediately when everyone leaves. These people are concerned about their reputation, but not so much about their character. Reputation is what you do in the light, when all eyes are on you, when the boss is there to pat you on the back, when your colleagues are there to watch you receive accolades. Character, on the other hand, is what you do in the dark, when everyone else has gone home, when the only light in the building is shining from your office, when you go home only after giving everything you have, without a timestamp letting everyone know you stayed late, but simply leaving your completed work, done to the best of your ability, on your desk. I wanted to earn my reputation by having a respectable, hard-working character. I believe if you are smart and work hard, success is inevitable.

I made a decision to pour myself into my work because my romantic relationships seemed temporary and fleeting, whereas my work produced consistent, permanent results. Still, I knew that one day I wanted to be in a solid relationship, and I worried about the same things that many women do. I worried that I wasn't doing something right. As I gained success within my career, I found that many men were intimidated by me. They saw me as competition or either an opportunity, instead of a companion. In addition to that, when I did find someone suitable to date, I found it difficult to take the proverbial pants off in my personal life.

After unsuccessfully dating a few guys in my industry, I started to question even my own intentions. Why was I starting to exclusively date men of a certain caliber or of a certain occupation? Was I dating them out of convenience, familiarity or only because of their success? As I started asking myself these questions, I decided to expand my dating territory. There was an attractive guy who worked for FedEx that routinely delivered packages to my office. We would often exchange a few flirty looks and glances, but I could tell he was too intimidated to speak. One day, I decided to work up my confidence and give it a shot. I politely spoke and said we should grab dinner one day after work, if he's free, and slipped him my business card. He followed up a few days later, told me the date and time of our dinner and chose, Asia de Cuba, one of the most expensive restaurants in town. The dinner conversation went a little something like this:

Guy: You look very nice tonight.

Me: Thank you, so do you. How was your day?

Guy: It was hard, but you know, I do manual labor. Something you don't know anything about.

Me: (Awkward laugh) Well, I'm sure we both work hard, so I'm glad we could finally take some time to get to know one another.

Guy: So, what's it like working for Russell Simmons?

Me: It's amazing! He's a great boss.

Guy: Balling (Jim Jones voice)!!!

Me: *Confused*

Guy: What you make...like six figures?

Me: I do okay.

Guy: Balling (Jim Jones voice again)!!! So, where do you live?

Me: In midtown around 37th and 9th.

Guy: Balling!!!!!!!!

Needless to say, our dinner soon ended, but not before him sliding the check over in my direction and telling me to pay for it. This was the first time in my life that I had begun to witness the evidence of my own power and the seemingly threating potential of my own success. When I looked in the mirror each day, I still saw the small town girl. I still saw the unpaid intern and didn't realize the way the outside world viewed me was starting to shift. And I wasn't ready to play small or give up any amount of power or control to anyone. As much as I wanted companionship, I had worked too hard and I enjoyed having complete control in my life.

A young woman striving to climb any career ladder will be tested, and especially so in the entertainment industry. When you are attractive and ambitious, it is assumed that you are sexually loose or easy and that your primary aim is not career satisfaction, but to be wifed up by an entertainer or someone in the executive ranks of the industry. It is not a possibility that you will be tested in this way; it is a certainty. I was not immune to being tested. One of the most public and embarrassing moments of my life began in this way. In no way was I easy or loose, but despite my title, accomplishments, and work ethic, I was still a woman who hoped to one day find someone who loved and adored her. While climbing the ranks within the Hip-Hop Summit Action Network, I became reacquainted with an old friend, who had become a well-known rapper. He took me out to dinner. He professed that he had always loved me. I let him down gently. He then proceeded to have beautiful bouquets of fragrant flowers sent to my office every day for about a month. Every single day.

There were so many flowers that I began redirecting them to people that I was trying to meet and build working relationships with throughout the entertainment industry. He sent handwritten cards with declarations of love. Eventually, he won me over. I wanted to move slowly and cautiously. He agreed. A few weeks later, he presented me with a 19-carat diamond ring and a proposal of marriage. Despite my gut feeling that I should not accept, I said yes – but under the condition that we have a long engagement and take some more time to get to know each other in this way. However, in the weeks that followed, I remained uneasy about the relationship. Things were moving too fast, yet every weekend I caught a red-eye to be wherever he was. On one of those weekends, he put me on the phone with one of his friends. We chatted and had a great, very casual conversation. By the time we hung up, I felt that I had made a new friend. A few weeks into the engagement, as I walked through Grand Central Station on my way to work, I noticed a picture of me on the cover of a magazine. I picked it up, and read words from me and by me, but that sounded nothing like me. As I read the byline, I realized that the "friend" was actually a journalist. I was angry, but more than that, I was hurt and felt betrayed by people I'd trusted. Who had I become? How could my professional life be in such order, but my personal life in such a mess? I felt that all the hard work and effort I had put into building my career were for naught. How in the hell had I been so stupid? I had to explain the situation to my family and friends. I had to endure what felt like a never-ending news cycle of scrutiny in the media. I was defeated. I went from the behind-the-scenes executive to in front of the camera. I wanted to give up. Still, I went in to work every day. I still maintained my standard of excellence with regard to my career, but my reputation had taken a huge hit. And I very quietly placed that ginormous diamond ring in a plain FedEx package, and shipped it back to its owner.

I refused to bring the talk about my personal life into the office setting. My colleagues tried to make it office conversation, but I continued to shut it down. My boss took notice. Despite the adversity and negative press I endured, I was eventually promoted again. One day, Russell and I were alone on an elevator ride back up to the 43rd floor. He asked me how my fiancé was doing. I told him it was over. As the doors opened, he said, "That's what you get," and walked off.

CHAPTER NINE

Take the Stairs

*"If you can't figure out your purpose, figure out your passion.
For your passion will lead you directly to your purpose."*

– Unknown

These days, the value that society places on money and fame would have you believe that a once-embarrassing video is now a quick pass to success. Even though reality television, Hollywood, and social media paint a picture that InstaFame now trumps ethics and morals, this is simply not the case. Class and grace never go out of style. They will always be relevant. Making a sex tape may make you relevant for a moment, but you will spend a lifetime amping up shock value in order to stay in the limelight. You will not be known for your hard work and dedication to your career and purpose. If anything, being filmed in a compromising situation can detract from it. However, mistakes are inevitable. Everyone has a turn (or several) at making a bad decision. It doesn't mean you're a bad person. You're just human. However, in order to turn a mess into a message, you have to acknowledge it. Then you have to grow up. Re-dedicate yourself to your purpose. Vow to be better every day than you were the day before. Everyone has to figure out his or her boundaries, but it is especially important at the beginning of your career, when the work-life balance is basically non-existent. That is how you overcome.

During this time, two life-changing events occurred. One was the stepping-stone to the project I hold most dear – the formation of the Women in Entertainment Empowerment Network, or WEEN. I had always known I wanted to empower and inspire women in some way. Growing up in North Carolina, the only glamorous women we were exposed to, especially in the entertainment realm, were on television and in movies. We set our standards based on those concepts of beauty. Because of this, my friends and I often wondered if we were smart enough, pretty enough, sassy enough, or sexy enough to be admired and acknowledged the way the young women in films, television, and music videos were.

The opportunity arose when Oprah hosted an on-air Hip Hop Town Hall and invited Kevin Liles, Dr. Benjamin Chavis, Common and Russell on as panelists. In the wake of the racist and insensitive remarks made by shock jock Don Imus towards the Rutgers women's basketball team by calling them "nappy-headed hoes," Imus cleverly redirected the dialogue to the misogynistic undertone of the entertainment industry.

The panel, including my boss, came under attack by the audience, a group of Spelman students brought in by satellite and the world-at-large for the reckless way women, especially African-American women were portrayed in the media. Immediately after that interview, I knew that more had to be done. Not a single African-American woman in the entertainment industry was represented on any of those talk shows or roundtables. Essentially, we had no voice. I organized a meeting for Russell soon after at the home of Lyor Cohen, one of the most powerful men in the entertainment industry. At the table sat the power players in the business. They were mostly men. They were over 50. I sat along the wall and listened to the conversation. The conversation centered on young women of color, how they were portrayed in the media, and how the young women of color who watched it were responding. I remember thinking, *They are talking about me. I should say something.* One of my biggest regrets is that I said nothing in that room. I allowed people who could not directly identify with my demographic make powerful decisions on my behalf simply because I didn't recognize my own power. I was on the bottom of the totem pole in that room, and didn't feel that my voice mattered. I knew that every meeting would be like this one. Other meetings would have a person with smart, powerful ideas who would be silenced because of position. Those ideas needed to be heard. With Russell's blessing, I struck out to gauge the landscape directly from the source – young women.

I organized a meeting with a few of the most powerful women in entertainment. From there, I prepared a proposal for WEEN and submitted it to Russell. The program got the green light, and we went to work. We got the word out about what we wanted to do with the organization, and encouraged women to come out to support our cause. I originally predicted that 20-30 women would attend, and invited everyone to my house. However, more and more women heard about it, and began to RSVP. I had to find a larger venue. At our first meeting, one hundred and twenty women showed up. Recent college graduates and CEOs sat in the room together. The conversation about young women now included young women. In that meeting, I saw the need and the urgency required for us to make an impact on how women are viewed. I realized that this was not just an ordinary meeting; it was the beginning of a movement. From there, we organized closed-door meetings on different college campuses and sought the opinions of women on how we could provide a more balanced portrayal of ourselves in the media. However, I quickly tired of having a closed door. It was time to open up the floor to all women and have their voices heard. Along with my friends, Sabrina Thompson, Kristi Henderson and Lauren Lake, we began planning our first summit. We secured a venue that held 4,000 people and got the word out. I prayed that the event would be successful, but I didn't know what to expect. I just hoped that we weren't thinking too big, and that the program would not be a flop. On the day of the event, I woke up and looked out the window. It was raining. My stomach started to churn. People do not typically show up when the weather is bad. However, when I arrived at the venue four hours early to prepare, the sight I was greeted with lifted my spirits. Women were lined up for nearly four New York City avenues, with umbrellas and rain ponchos, waiting to get in. Not only did we fill the venue to capacity, but had to turn people away. I knew we were on to something special.

Have you had an opportunity to voice your opinion, but did not? In what ways can you convey the power of your opinion?

_____

_____

_____

_____

_____

The second life-changing event was brought about by being forced to attend a political event at a Mercedes Benz car dealership in Manhattan. After working all day, the last place I wanted to be that evening was in a showroom full of cars. I just felt it was a strange place to have a political rally. It was a small gathering of people. There were perhaps only

50-75 people in attendance. The rally was in support of Congressman Harold Ford, Jr., a young, charismatic political mind from Tennessee. Congressman Ford was the star of the evening and we were all there to support him. As I begrudgingly walked into the event, someone grabbed my arm to make an introduction. As I approached this unfamiliar face, he was introduced to me as freshman Senator Barack Obama. We shook hands and in that five-minute conversation we spoke about the impact young people would have on the next election, the need for real change in our country and building a coalition of young people. I was impressed by his passion and genuine love and concern for our nation, having no idea of his intentions to one day run for President of the United States.

"The true measure of a man is how he treats someone who can do him absolutely no good."

– Samuel Johnson

I worked hard for everything I had, and worked harder to maintain it and allow it to grow. I was very fulfilled in my position, but I still longed for more. I had grown up around public servants, and it had become a part of me that I needed to explore. They say the apple doesn't fall too far from the tree and while I never subscribed to that, I hungered to become more politically involved. Perhaps it was due in part to my parent's legacy, but I also saw the huge gap in the civic engagement of young people and knew somehow I could make a difference.

The young senator I had met at Rep. Harold Ford's campaign rally decided it was time for him to run for President of the United States. In addition to working for Russell, I began working for him, unpaid, at the end of 2006 as a volunteer. Only people who were politically educated knew who he was. He had an unusual name, Barack Obama, but not a widely recognizable one. He was unknown among celebrities. And to top it off, his primary competition was Hillary Clinton, one-half of a political dynasty. The odds were stacked against us. As volunteers, our job was to help him build his brand. I used what I had learned in my career to help. I began to leverage my assets, including the celebrity relationships I had established through my work with Russell, to help Barack Obama. I gave my pitch over the phone to anyone who was willing to listen as to why they should support him. I did whatever I needed to do, and called whomever I needed to call to assist this young man in becoming the President of the United States.

In 2008, the race was particularly tight in the state of Ohio. I knew that we had to find a way to set him apart and encourage young people to vote. At the time, LeBron James' Nike contract alone was worth more than ninety million dollars and I was trying to convince him, an Ohio native and certified NBA superstar, to host a rally in Ohio – for free. I was persistent, and when he finally agreed and I saw the successful execution of that event, I realized I had found another niche for myself. I began doing surrogate work – persuading celebrities and influencers to support and endorse political candidates and social causes.

It was an uphill battle. Our core target demographic, African-Americans, Caucasian-Americans, and senior citizens were very skeptical. They just didn't feel like it was his time. We turned to the group who was least likely to vote, least likely to care, but most likely to energize the base and started a movement. Young people built public awareness and the brand of Barack Obama brick by brick. The President stands on the solid foundation of those bricks today as he leads our country. Through volunteering for the Obama campaign, I clearly saw how celebrities could hold credible and measurable weight in the political process. The celebrities rallied young voters, and young voters rallied behind the President.

I was all in, win or lose, until the very end. I didn't do it to get a job. I had a job with Russell that I still loved and that now paid me very well. I didn't have ulterior motives. I simply wanted to help this man get elected. However, in the midst of the campaign, the economy took a major nosedive. We were suddenly in a recession, and my life and career changed drastically. My department in Russell's office, without warning, started losing many of its major sponsors as they began conserving their resources to weather the worsening economy. We went from raising millions a year to only a fraction of that. The very difficult decision was made to let go of our staff and I had to personally look them in their eyes and lay many of them off one-by-one. In solidarity and in order for the company to survive, I cut my own salary by 50%. I stayed with the company for as long as I could, but I was unable to maintain my bills and lifestyle on just half of my original income. I made the tough decision to leave.

I took a position in Chicago with the Alzheimer's Association. My grandmother had recently been diagnosed, and being a part of that non-profit allowed me to learn more about her disease. The environment was far different than the one I left. This job was about as typically corporate America as it gets. However, taking the job offered the return of the salary to which I was accustomed, and an amazing penthouse off Michigan Avenue that looked as if it was ripped from a magazine. I also gained the credibility of having a strictly corporate position as opposed to the entertainment industry, which many people did not take seriously. Once again, I began to encounter the traps of climbing in my career, but this time it came from an entry-level employee who just did not feel that someone who had worked in the entertainment industry, and specifically with hip-hop artists, had a place with their organization. He started rumors about people that I hung around with even though I barely knew him and never discussed my personal life with him. He contacted HR and told them that I did not follow procedure when allowing people into my office, which was not true. He then suggested that my friend, a public school teacher, was possibly a thug with gang affiliations. Nothing could be further from the truth. It was all resolved, but I took note that he only got the slightest of reprimands despite his disgusting actions. This version of corporate politics was far nastier than what I endured before. Throughout this upheaval of my life, I continued volunteering on the Obama campaign.

On the night before the election, my dad and I drove down to Charlotte to hear our soon-to-be President speak. Senator Obama's grandmother had passed away earlier that day. It was cold, and pouring down rain. After he spoke, we were allowed to go to the back greenroom to greet him. We were taking pictures, and this man, who would make history the next evening as the first African-American President-Elect of the United States, walked in my direction, gave me a hug and thanked me for my support. I simply said, "Sir, it was an honor." At that moment, I felt that I had been paid in full. For me, 'thank you' was enough.

"Generosity is the habit of giving without expecting anything in return."

– Wikipedia

Two months later, I traveled to Washington for the inauguration of the 44th President of the United States, Barack Hussein Obama. It was freezing cold. People were wearing layers of coats and jackets. Pop-up street vendors were selling overpriced hand and foot warmers. The restaurants surrounding Capitol Hill were overflowing with people trying to purchase a cup of coffee or tea to warm their numb bodies. The streets were full of people wanting to be a part of this historic moment, a moment created by young people. I remember the pride I felt that day, the power of knowing that this was a moment that I helped create in some small way. To see that, to know that we are capable of creating our own great moments, is such a powerful realization.

Having decided to freeze for fashion, I was dressed in four-inch heels with no gloves and no hat. I was carrying an All-Access Pass and getting ready to enjoy the day. As I prepared to get in place, my dear Uncle Toby Fitch, a judge and my father's former law partner, came up in his wheelchair to say hello. He and my father had worked on civil rights cases in North Carolina for decades, and he was basking in this day. I realized, even though young people created this moment, people like my

Uncle Toby and my dad created the foundation that made the moment possible. I gave him my All-Access Pass, stopped in a nail salon to get some Styrofoam slippers and joined the millions of people who had forever-changed the course of American history. We laughed, we cried and we danced together on the National Mall for hours. The feeling in the air that day will live with me forever.

Soon after the inauguration, I was back to my normal routine. In the office, as I returned from lunch, my cell phone started to ring.

"Ms. Butterfield, on behalf of the White House, we are calling to ask whether you would be interested in serving in the Administration of President Barack Obama?"

This can't be life. This can't be my life. Not only does our country have its first Black President, I've now been asked to serve in his Administration. Hold up. Me? Really? The range of emotions I felt in that moment will live with me for the rest of my life. Those words and what they meant rocked my world. Even though my job offered me the perks and benefits of a very comfortable life, I could not pass up the opportunity to work for this President, someone I believed in and worked so hard to help get elected. I left my penthouse and my cushy salary, and went to live with my dad in a cramped, no-frills, very basic apartment in DC.

To some, it looked like a step down, but to me it felt like another step forward. My new position required top-secret security clearance, and I had to go through a series of five or six interviews. In addition, about forty people closest to me were interviewed, and the details of my past were thoroughly vetted. I never thought that a tattoo I got at seventeen years old in the (literally) one-stoplight town of Elm City, NC would be a topic for security clearance. However, I was required to take note of and explain any distinguishing marks on my body. Nothing was off limits. It was an extremely humbling experience.

All of my mistakes, all of the trials that I faced in my life were scrutinized. Through that experience, I learned that how you conduct yourself, and the decisions you make, create a footprint that lives with you forever. I also learned that people and potential employers are willing to forgive your mistakes as long as you are honest about them and can show that you have grown as a result. I also learned that no one expected me to be perfect. None of us are. Flaws and failure come with the territory of building a successful life. The only way they can destroy us is in our refusal to acknowledge them. It is vital to forgive yourself and stand in your truth so you can move forward in the bright future that awaits you.

This was a proud moment in my life. My commitment to service had paid off in an unexpected way. I was proud that I earned this political nod on my own. My parents, often times on my journey, told me they would not call in special favors on my behalf or for my professional advancement. At times, I was angry and resentful, not understanding the true value in becoming a woman and valued professional in my own right. However, in the wake of that life-changing phone call, I fully realized that my parents were building me up by allowing me to know my strength, my work ethic, and my commitment to excellence were enough. While I am extremely proud of the legacy created by my parents and grandparents, and the "good" name they have given to our family, I am happy that instead of having to hide behind the name to accomplish my goals, I have been able to add to the legacy with my own works and achievements.

It wasn't until I started working for the Obama Administration, and became a public servant myself that I started to fully realize the sacrifice that my parents made in choosing careers of service to others. When I was young, I took their positions for granted. There were moments when I didn't realize how necessary, how absolutely vital, their service was in the growth and development of our community. When they sometimes spent more time away from home instead of with my sister and me, doing things that we heard other families did, I felt twinges of resentment towards the "job" and the people who took my parents away from me. Yet somehow, their diligence and steadfast devotion to serving others became a part of me as well. Even as I worked for opportunities in the entertainment business, sprinkles of service always managed to infiltrate and impact my life.

My job with the Obama Administration was just the continuation of a ride I'd been on for a long time. I came into a department that was divided between the political appointees and the long-term federal employees. I realized very early on that the long-term employees had watched people like me come and go through several administrations, and that I would get nothing accomplished by throwing around my position and title. They were ready to wait me out until the next appointee came in. The atmosphere had to change in order to accomplish the work that we were all there to do. I let them know that I needed them, I valued their experience and voice, and I was there to work on behalf of the citizens of the United States. When you let people know that you recognize their value, they are willing to work with you to accomplish the objectives that have been set. As a team, we were able to revamp a website that had not been updated in ten years within six months. Because everyone was treated with respect and their opinion valued, not only did we meet expectations, but exceeded them. I was able to work at the federal level to make the country better and give everyone a chance to achieve the American dream. I had come full circle.

What do you think are the hallmarks of a great leader?

_____

_____

_____

_____

_____

One of the best parts of working for the Administration was the opportunity to spend time with one of the most powerful people in the world – Michelle Obama. Our First Lady is the epitome of loveliness and grace. She is everything I ever envisioned our first African-American First Lady to be. She is smart, stylish, and sassy. She honors God and puts her family first. Every chance I got to be in the presence of Michelle Obama was an opportunity that never got old. I've learned so much from her, not the least of which is learning to serve with dignity, grace, and class.

By working on different levels of service, from local to national, I have learned that you don't always have to go to a big city with flashing lights to make a major impact with your work. There is intrinsic value in being a large fish in a smaller pond. It gives you an opportunity to perfect your craft, create a buzz and develop a loyal following.

My dad is a prime example. He used his law degree to go back to his hometown and fight local and state civil rights cases that directly affected his neighbors and community. It took time, but the community showed their appreciation for his service by electing him as a Superior Court judge, a NC Supreme Court judge, and eventually, as a

United States Congressman. He now works at the federal level, but is ever mindful that he is the voice for his hometown and his community.

When you invest in your community, your community will invest in you. They will rally behind you and be your biggest cheerleaders. If you desire to reach a national or even international audience, they will help you propel to that stage. I am reminded of the old saying "Do not despise small beginnings." Don't be so focused on making a big impact that you fail to make an impact at all. Bloom where you are planted.

How can you make an impact in your community?

_____

_____

_____

_____

_____

_____

However, if you choose to do it my way know that it too is possible. When you travel to a major city, your goal should never be to "get discovered" or spotted. Your clear goal should be to go get what is rightfully yours. Your dreams are non-negotiable and you are your only competition. Don't start the habit of comparing your journey to the next woman's journey or comparing what she has materially to your own. This is your path and if you traveled to New York City, Los Angeles, London, Johannesburg or any other major city, that is exactly where you are supposed to be. But faith and purpose, while valid, are not enough. You must put in the work. You must be strategic. And you must be willing to sacrifice to get what you want.

"Faith without works is dead."
– James 2:17

If your aim is to climb the social ladder, I'll tell you now, the entertainment industry and a life of service is probably not for you. As glamorous as the entertainment industry or even working for the President seems, it is far from that and a lot of hard work. You are constantly being tried and put to the test to see if you are professionally who you say you are. And once you've proven your value, you will then be expected to work twice as hard and three times as smart.

Service is also not for everyone and that's okay. We are all built to do different things. Don't be afraid to *own your truth*, and to build your life around it. You can always give back in small ways, or donate money and resources to worthy causes. You cannot fake service. It is too time-consuming. It is too draining. The people who are not truly committed always fall off eventually.

Service can be a very lonely vocation. It will make you wonder who is investing in you as you spend your life investing in others. It is vital that you serve where you see a need and have a passion. Passion must be directly related to service so you can be spiritually fed while helping others. Also, know that you can't help anyone when you are broke or broken. A life of service does not mean you are destined to a life of poverty. I certainly did not take a vow of poverty and neither should you. You deserve to have someone or something that gives to you spiritually, emotionally, and financially. You have to make sure the deposits of spirit, time and treasure are at least equal to the withdrawals of the same that you give. Otherwise, you will face a deficit. Your life will not be in balance. You will no longer be helping people, and you will be turned off from living a life of service. There is nothing wrong with saving for home ownership as you help the homeless. There is nothing wrong with saving for retirement as you help the elderly with their needs. I am telling you from experience. You must also remember to serve yourself.

If you are a college student with a normal job making minimal money, but you try to volunteer with every organization and give to every worthy cause, you'll find soon enough that your homework suffers, your GPA suffers, and your job suffers. None of these things should be compromised for the sake of a false sense of generosity. *No* is a powerful and necessary word. *No* keeps you from exceeding your capacity to uphold your commitments. *No* keeps you from burning out your brain and your body. *No* is a complete sentence. People will try to convince you to say yes. They will ask for a four-page letter detailing why you are denying them of what belongs to *you*. You don't owe them an explanation. Don't get caught in that trap, because if you offer an explanation, it won't be good enough for them anyway. *No* is a word of self-protection, and it is a word that protects the service you have already committed to give. Learn to say *no* with a smile. It doesn't have to be nasty. It comes from a place of love. The people who are asking don't really want you if you can't offer your best, and you have to be at your best to move your passion and purpose forward.

You become a leader in your community through your service. That leadership is derived from a place of true passion and purpose in your life. Leaders are not the loudest people in the room. Leaders humbly, quietly, and effectively move the cause forward. True leaders are not nasty, they are not aggressive, and they are not demanding. There is a wealth of value in being the quiet storm. Create a strategy with both your words and your silence, but most importantly your *actions*. Be selective as you choose your words. Never let them see you sweat.

Know that working in service, you will encounter losses as well as wins. People will not always treat you kindly. Programs won't always run as planned. Colleagues will let you down. The person you want to help the most will reject all of your offers. This is all a part of the process. Just know that your service extends to your defeats, and how you choose to handle them. Show grace, class and dignity in a loss, and you will gain ground. There is no room for bad attitudes and negativity in servant leadership. Fight against the stereotypes. Prove your naysayers wrong by maintaining an element of professionalism that cannot be misconstrued. Support your words with hard data and facts. Play the game to win, because when you win, so do the people and causes you are serving.

Take the time to learn who you are, and take that into your role as a servant leader. Your personality should be infused in your position. No one can handle your job quite like you. Do not be afraid to take a risk and stand out, especially in a way that is organic to your personality. This is why their organization wants you versus every other candidate they interviewed. Your personal "it factor" is what sets you apart from the pack.

CHAPTER TEN

The Discovery

I grew up in church. My relationship with God and my foundation within the church are very closely related. However, one day in the midst of serving others, I realized that I had not been to church in almost a year. I'd begun a pattern of reciting routine prayers before each meal and before going to bed each night, without nurturing my relationship with God. I was talking at God instead of having a conversation with Him. God had become an afterthought. The job and the trappings of my life had taken over almost completely. I longed to once-again have an active and open prayer life. I longed to be a part of people who believed as I did, that if we seek God first, that all things would be added unto you. I began making time for what truly mattered to me.

By reconnecting with God, I made an important discovery. I realized that I prayed every night for God to forgive me of mistakes that I had made long, long ago. I consistently apologized for those mistakes, and as I lived longer and made more mistakes, I added them to the list. Finally, as I prayed one evening, God assured me that I had been forgiven the first time I asked, and that He had let all of my mess go at that moment. The only person holding on was me. I had to forgive myself. I had to give myself permission to let those mistakes stay firmly in the past where they belonged. God is all-powerful, all mighty, and all knowing, and if He says it's over, then it is. I was out helping everybody else, but I had to re-learn, or perhaps, learn for the first time, how to invest in myself. I wasn't taking proper care of my spirit, time or treasure. Once I realized that I had to take care of me in order to serve in the most effective way, I began guarding my spirit, time and treasure fiercely, so I could do more. You can't be generous with a dry well.

When you have a family, you have to become even more diligent in creating boundaries as you work in service to others. When I first started working for Russell, it crossed my mind that if he didn't live such a lavish lifestyle, he could help more people. However, when I began to see the sheer amount of requests that came in for financial assistance for various individuals and organizations, I quickly learned that even if he gave his last dime, he would not be able to help everyone. Setting limits not only ensures that he can provide he and his family with the lifestyle he planned for them to have, but also that there is a consistent flow of money to give to the individuals and causes he chooses. Earmarking both your money and your time protects your interests, as well as the interests of those you serve.

After traveling around the world and experiencing things this small town girl could have never imagined, while traveling back from a trip to Liberia and the Sudan one morning, as we arrived at Andrews Air Force Base, I felt so full yet so alone. I realized that my life over the last ten years had gone by so fast and I had no one to look back and share those memories with. My hard climb up was met with loneliness and a longing for someone to share my life with. My current relationship wasn't heading towards marriage and I was ready to settle down. My dear friend Adonis called me one day and said he had someone for me to meet. While intrigued, when he told me his name and that he played professional basketball, I started to proceed with caution. At this point, I'd dated guys in the limelight before and felt it was time for me to depart from that lifestyle. Dahntay and I had been introduced two years prior by email, but never met face-to-face. Each time he invited me to dinner, I somehow found an excuse. But not this time. I was ready and open to meet someone new. It began with a few phone calls and led to a first meeting over lunch in New York City. I was the first to arrive at the restaurant with my hair in a ponytail and no make-up, but when I saw this six foot six man with a perfect smile walk into the restaurant, I made a mad dash to the restroom to get glammed up. My heart felt butterflies it hadn't felt in years. He said very little and I probably said too much over that four hour lunch, but we've been together ever since.

I appreciated his kind heart and gentle nature, as well as the fact that he got to know me after the lavish lifestyle, the six-figure salary, the penthouse and the car service. I was a public servant living in a run-down apartment, by choice. He would have to love me for me. Likewise, he found it refreshing to be with a woman who was committed to her own career and was not impressed with his money or status as a professional basketball player. I knew from our first date that he was the one for me. I knew that our relationship, and what we built within it, was not for public consumption.

We were engaged in ten months and married in just under two years. My marriage and the building of my family had to become the priority in my life. God is first, and my family is second. If public service trumped either of them, I would be out of order and nothing would thrive. I knew that I wanted to live in the same house with my husband, and that meant I had to resign from my position with the Obama Administration. I had mixed emotions, but knew I had made the correct decision. However, within weeks of my resignation and wedding, I got another call from the White House. They needed my unique services for President Obama's reelection campaign, and wanted to bring me on-board as the National Youth Vote Director. The position was a dream opportunity for me. I got to spend time engaging young people, promoting awareness of the political process, and persuading young people to get registered to vote and to the polls. I talked it over with my brand new husband, and accepted the position. However, I had a few caveats. I needed to leave early on Fridays (which, during a campaign, leaving early on any day is unfathomable). I needed to go home to my husband on weekends. My newly-formed family had to come before the job. So I moved to Chicago, and drove three hours to Indianapolis on Friday evenings to be with Dahntay. The guards at the Indiana Pacers' stadium got so used to me that they bypassed protocol when they saw my car enter into the arena every weekend. The very untypical basketball wife that I had become, I would roll into games in Ugg boots, black leggings and with bags under my eyes the size of golf balls.

In the months that followed, Dahntay and I had yet another reason to make sure that we unapologetically made family our top priority. I was pregnant. I definitely didn't plan to get pregnant during election season, but it had happened. We knew it would be difficult, but we were thrilled. We just had to roll with the punches. I didn't tell anyone on the campaign staff that I was pregnant right away. I didn't want to be seen as irresponsible or unable to handle my position. However, after turning down countless offers to go have drinks with my colleagues coupled with my public bout of all-day sickness, I could no longer hide my pregnancy.

I don't know why I was worried. When I finally broke the news, the campaign staff rallied around me. We were a second family, and they treated me with the utmost concern and care as I continued to work throughout my pregnancy. When I went into labor with my son DJ, I continued replying to emails until almost the very moment he was born. But when I held my little miracle in my arms, life immediately went into focus.

CHAPTER ELEVEN

The Second Quarter (#NoFilter)

I feel that I have entered the best part of my life, the second quarter. I'm old enough to have learned some valuable life lessons, but still young enough to enjoy the benefits of my hard work. I am still ambitious, but I am also complete. I have a husband, a child, and the career of my dreams, and I worked damn hard to make it happen. I'm no longer in a position where I am trying to figure it out. The second quarter is about the execution of the purpose that I figured out in my twenties, and making sure it's as flawless and seamless as possible. I am working to be healthier physically, spiritually, and emotionally. I am working to be a better wife, mother, daughter, sister and friend. I can be a better person to others now, because I've learned to treat myself well and accept myself as I am, flaws and all.

Also, now that the foundation of my life is solid, I can say unapologetically that in this second quarter of my life, I want to be rich. I used to think it was very shallow and self-centered to want wealth, but I have learned that it's okay to have big financial goals and think wealthy. I have had a six-figure salary, and mismanaged all of my money. I learned through that experience that whether I have ninety dollars or ninety million, budgeting is a priority. No woman should carry around a designer purse, and have no money to put in it. Input must exceed output in order to grow true wealth.

Every now and then, the song "Money, Power, Respect" rings in my ears. Our nation is set-up as a capitalistic society. That means it takes *money* to help people, and my life is a testament to the importance of giving back. I have to make money if I want to fulfill my goal of servant leadership. The *power* is what I have seen working in D.C., observing lawmakers and policies that affect our future. And though *respect* has many forms, to me, my 94-year-old grandmother epitomizes respect. She has no accolades, no degrees, and no titles, but she has always lived her life honorably. I hold myself to a standard that requires respect first, then money, and finally, power.

I've learned so many things since embarking on this journey to live an authentic and unfiltered life.

"It takes 20 years to build a reputation
and five minutes to ruin it.
If you think about that, you'll do things differently."

– Warren Buffett

In the age of selfies and Instagram, the temptation to show, or in most cases exaggerate, your life's highlight reel can become overwhelming. When video vixens and booty models have 200,000 followers and the hard-working college student has around 250, it can cause even the best of us to reevaluate our priorities. But what I know for certain is there are no elevator rides to the top.

It can be discouraging when you're trying your best to build a solid career without compromising your integrity to watch women who look as if they live with their glam squad flooding the media through reality television and social media. While the idea of using television as a platform appeals to me, I am unyielding in my efforts to make sure it does not negate the years I've spent building a solid career and advocating the rights of women. Because of that, I've turned down several offers. I desire to have a global impact, but making a destructive decision in order to gain notoriety will not garner the results I seek. If I cannot promote a positive image of women, then I don't want to be a part of it.

Because of the connections I've made over the years, I have the opportunity to sit at exclusive dinners with impressive guest lists. After a while, you start to notice a pattern. All of the A-list celebrities are in the front of the room, people who have steady, if not flashy, careers sit in the middle, and the people who are just beginning (and very happy to be in the room at all) sit in the rear. I've been in the back of the room, and now I sit somewhere in the middle. I watch from the middle as the hot reality show celebrity sits in the front for a year or two, only to be replaced by the next hot reality celebrity when a new show airs or the new season begins. It's short-term, and while I may never sit in the front of the room, rest assured I will be *in* the room every single time. If I knew better when I was sitting in the back (or before I was ever invited), I would have been paying attention to the people in the middle. Often, they are the most powerful people in the room. Make sure your image and brand portrays the longevity you truly seek.

When being considered for a job, the good ole' social media scrub by an employer has become the norm. They are almost guaranteed to check your online behavior to determine your character and to ultimately gauge what your offline behavior will be in a place of business. If your pictures have more rear facing shots than not, or your page has more images of drunken nights than those in less compromising settings, you can rest assured that you will not land that job.

"You can't build a reputation on what you are going to do."

– Henry Ford

However, once you've landed the job, the real work to build and manage your reputation begins. Often, when you're the newbie on the job you can feel the entire office sizing you up. For some, you may be considered a threat, while to others you are considered fresh meat. This is all par for the course, but how you move and navigate it all will help determine your success.

The first rule that I created and adhered to on the job was to never sleep where you eat. In layman's terms, that means don't sleep around or screw your colleagues. Harsh words, but true. Regardless of how many Hallmark cards, flowers or love professing comes your way, don't do it. Ever.

Once a woman's reputation is tarnished it is almost irreparable while men ultimately get pats on the back and earn new stripes. Think about it, who wants to face an ex-boyfriend or, even worse, an ex-lover at the water cooler each day or on the elevator, especially when everyone knows – and they *will* find out. You want to be taken seriously as the professional young woman that you are and for your peers to see you without distractions.

The second rule is having a two-drink maximum in after-work settings. You never want your colleagues to see you out of character and you always need to be in control. While others get sloppy and distastefully drunk, maintain your cool and resist the pressure. They may want to drag you down and this is seemingly the perfect opportunity for you to give in.

Third, always remain the calm in the storm. In corporate settings and meetings, you often deal with Type A, high-strung personalities, which thrive in chaos and confusion. Adopt a drama-free approach to business and remain the voice of reason when madness strikes. Always find the solutions.

Finally, and most importantly, recognize that you are human and mistakes happen. You will not be perfect on this journey and you must deal with issues, as they come, head on.

Let's say for example, you screwed up, knocked down too many drinks and had a night you'd like to forget with Mike in marketing. When you return to work the next day, don't shrink, play small or let your regrets show. Quietly walk over to Mike and say, "Look, you and I both know we should leave last night in the past. We are mature enough to accept what it was and move on as colleagues and friends." If Mike moves on, great. If Mike yells it from a bullhorn in the office the next day, well, that's unfortunate, but leave that night and your conversation with him where it belongs – in the past – and move on. Your methodical silence will speak volumes. If you stay focused on your work, the Mikes of the world will lose interest fairly quickly and either move on or find a new target.

However, if the taunting continues, do not be afraid to report his badgering to Human Resources. Some people have to learn the hard way that you refuse to be pushed around.

"People only bring up your past when they are intimidated by your present."

– Unknown

On this journey, there will be haters, but most importantly, there will be support from people you least expect to offer it. Spend your time focusing less on the people who want to see you fail and more on developing allies in the people who are rooting for you. If there are two people who absolutely detest your existence and there are twenty people who want to see you win, your time is best spent investing in and forging relationships with people who support the vision you have for yourself. But relationships are give and take. You must be willing to give as much to the relationships you are nurturing as you are getting, or they too will fall apart.

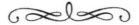

"I've learned that making a living is not the same thing as making a life."

– Maya Angelou

I'm proud of the success that I've earned. Moreover, I'm proud of how I earned it – honorably, through dedication and hard work. As you embark on your own endeavors, whether traditional or non-traditional, remember to honor yourself in your work. Let your work show that you believe in your talent, and that your talent is worth the hard work, the late hours, and the sacrifice. Honoring ourselves is critical to our success. It is a mandate of God. I'm beginning to learn that the process of loving yourself and embracing your beauty, including your flaws, is a journey and not a destination. Don't measure your worth by your number of followers or likes, but rather, develop true relationships that withstand the lows and highs of the paths you choose. Even the seemingly most confident people can fall victim to the pressure to keep up.

This pressure mounts into temptation to create shortcuts. The pressure can motivate us to either become our best or worst selves. Will our dreams become buried and invalid? Will we invite the pressure to become a part of our growing process? Or, will we allow the challenges that we will inevitably face to transform us, as we find and face our flaws in a lifelong quest, not for perfection, but to simply become better than we were yesterday? We must each take a path, specifically designed for us, in order to become successful. The beauty of *The Girlprint* is that your path will be uniquely yours, as my story is uniquely mine. However, I do hope you take heed to the lessons in my story and apply it to your life in a way that makes sense for you.

There are certain similarities we will face as women pursuing success in our current society. The revelation that we possess the capacity to be both powerful and bold, yet women of dignity is a game-changing idea, especially in the 21st century. Many women know how to do one well, but those who realize that the two concepts are not adversarial, but work in tandem, are the ladies who will ultimately rise to the top of their fields.

Who you are and what you are at this moment does not define you. Without diminishing the seriousness of any challenge you face, mistake you have made, or problem you have or will encounter, you must still stand firm in the absolute knowledge that the vision that refuses to die within you exists for a reason. No one can see it through exactly like you. Many times people will say that you were created to serve out your vision, and that the fruition of that service will, in turn, serve others. This is true. However, have you ever thought that you were broken for your vision as well?

You were hurt, you were tried, you suffered or were shamed to give perspective and a heart for others as you heal and build better. You failed, sometimes repeatedly, perhaps epically, in order to learn how to fight, climb, and persevere. Sometimes, we must be broken and rebuilt so that through our cracks, those places that could not be brought together no matter the strength of the glue, God's light can shine through us and show others how the Creator works in us and through us. Who do you want to be? What is your passion? Write it down. If you are afraid, write it afraid. Bravery is not the absence of fear; it is the conquering of fear. Write down your purpose and put it up in a place where you have to constantly see it and remind yourself that your path is much more important than your perceived failures along the way.

The more we can be honest about who we are and our beginnings, no matter how humble, the more we allow our purpose to reach deeper depths, and ultimately, higher heights. Unfortunately, filtering has become our status quo. We filter our words before we hit the update button on Facebook. We filter our pictures, cropping out the unattractive parts, creating the intended mood, showing ourselves in the best possible light, all before we share. In order to become truly successful, we must unlearn our filtering techniques.

That does not mean that we should be crude or crass. It doesn't even mean that we have to show every pimple and scar. But it does mean that we have to show some. We have to be willing to acknowledge our shortcomings, because the fabric of our story is in our testimony. We connect with one another through our weakness and vulnerability. True change agents know that there is inspiration for others in our darkest moments.

Whatever you choose to do professionally, allow some scars to show. Let the world know that you're still here, and that you lived through your trials.

Discarding our filters takes time. It takes an acute awareness of self. Take the time to figure *who* you are, before exploring *what* you want to do. Take the time to work with your flaws to accomplish something on your own terms. The same way you must become acquainted with your weaknesses, you must also become acquainted with your strengths. You have to find out how both sides of the equation work in your life. If you don't find your personal equilibrium, you are subject to start believing your own hype. You will start to believe that you are the version of yourself that you have been showing to everyone. You will believe you are handling things, when the reality is there are messy items that you have conveniently cropped out. However, they are still there. You will give too much of self, and not require what is necessary to make you whole. Therefore, you must get to know your naked, exposed self first.

What can you do without the crutch of your parents, your friends, or (especially) your significant other? In fact, I will go so far as to say that until you truly know yourself, you shouldn't seek a partner. Why would you bring someone else into your messy, mixed-up life, layered with filters, and cropped until the real you is recognized? Eventually, the filters will fade, and that person will begin to see the rest of the picture. And if the whole, jacked-up, unfiltered picture of you is not something that you can embrace alone, then you certainly should not try to sell it to someone else. I'm not telling you to perfect your mess, but you must accept it. Clean what you can. Create a complete picture you can be proud of, by yourself and for yourself. Once you do that, you'll be able to invite someone else to peruse your selfie albums.

I honestly feel that this is what we should do in our twenties. We should take the time to feel our power as adults, and learn about ourselves in respect to the real world and not the sheltered version many of our parents gave to us. Too many young women are more concerned about getting married, or having a pretty wedding, than with becoming a good partner to themselves. I was once one of them. You have to know who you are without the filter and learn to love that flawed, imperfect person who will keep staring at you in the mirror until your last day on earth. Truly loving yourself is a process, often painful and slow. When you cheat yourself out of the process, you usually end up linking up with someone else who hasn't learned to love themselves and is unable to love you the way you deserve. Marriage is selfless. It is a life-long commitment to give your love, your time, your support, and your body. It is a full-time job, and there are no days off. How can you effectively do that when you haven't given that to yourself first? Shouldn't you be the first partaker in your love and time? And how can you make a vow before God when you haven't sought God out as a single person? Why would you make a promise to a stranger?

Take the time to be selfish. Selfishly seek a relationship with God. Let Him guide you in your purpose. Work tirelessly while your only true responsibility is you. Throw out every checklist about finding the perfect partner. Stop reciting crazy relationship rules you read in an old *Cosmopolitan* at the dentist's office. Have fun. Choose your partners wisely, and date freely. Do not settle down until you figure yourself out. However, never forget that you are the CEO of your personal brand, and the people you choose to spend time with are a reflection of your brand. Proceed with caution, and live out loud and without regret. I know that you have what it takes to succeed. It is already inside of you. It just requires activation. Just know that you are exactly where you need to be to get started. You don't have to be in New York or Los Angeles. Start where you are. Begin your journey by beginning the process of your own revelation. Don't let anyone deter you from achieving the greatness that is already planted in your heart. President Barack Obama once said, "I have always believed that hope is that stubborn thing inside of us that insists, despite all the evidence to the contrary, that something better awaits us so long as we have the courage to keep reaching, to keep working, to keep fighting." Treat every day as if it is another stepping-stone to success. Wake up ready to have your purpose actualized. Do not settle for being anything less than unapologetically, imperfectly great.

Acknowledgments

At the risk of omitting a single person of the countless who have paved the way, let me begin by apologizing in advance. Charge my head and not my heart.

To my mom, my biggest fan, who has spoken up for me to the point of embarrassment, who defended me, at times, when I didn't deserve it and who has loved me unconditionally every step of the way. I owe everything to you and more. As a mom, I get it now and I am eternally grateful and love you to the moon and back. To my dad, as a daddy's girl, you set such a high bar for me professionally that there were times when I wasn't sure I could amount. Thank you for giving me the foundation, the encouragement and motivation to challenge myself and to defy the odds. I'm made from good stuff and it is because I stand on your shoulders. To my grandmother, Odell Sharpe Farmer, you are my rock. You taught me how to be a loyal wife, a loving mom and most importantly, a good woman. You are my backbone and the legacy upon which I proudly stand.

Without my Heirlight family, this book would not exist – James Artis, my day one manager who started in the trenches with me more than a decade ago, we did it! Alexandra Blanton, thank you for putting up with my late night emails and texts and always responding with class and grace. LaMonique Hamilton, not only are you the co-author of this book, our friendship has withstood the test of time – you simply are the best and I'm so glad the world can experience what you have to offer. To my master editor, Karen Thomas, who does her job with lightening speed and accuracy, thank you.

To Russell Simmons, JoJo Brim, Kevin Liles and Dr. Benjamin Chavis, thank you for being my guardian angels, always taking my late night phone calls and helping me navigate one of the most competitive industries in the world. You are the blueprint.

To my husband, Dahntay Jones. You are the sole reason that I could take a few months off to write my first book. Thank you for believing in me. Thank you for loving me. Your faith, your patience, your grace – I learn from each and every day. I love you, LOML.

Finally, to my baby boy, Dahntay Laval Jones, Jr. You are the reason I exist. Through your life, I now know the reason for my own. I'm going to give you every ounce of me to prepare you for life and to be the best person you can be, both personally and professionally. I love you, My Sunnie.